The Origins of
American Intervention in
the First World War

THE NORTON ESSAYS IN AMERICAN HISTORY

Under the general editorship of

HAROLD M. HYMAN

William P. Hobby Professor of American History
Rice University

The Origins of
American Intervention in
the First World War

Ross Gregory

W · W · NORTON & COMPANY

New York · London

W. W. Norton & Company, Inc., 500 Fifth Avenue, New York, N.Y. 10110
W. W. Norton & Company Ltd., 25 New Street Square, London EC4A 3NT

Library of Congress Catalog Card No. 70-141588

ISBN 0-393-09980-6

9 0

For my mother

Contents

Preface

THE FIRST WORLD WAR was a gigantic landmark in the history of mankind. In a real sense it was the beginning of the twentieth century and what we call modern times. It destroyed or weakened many of those forces that had fashioned the world for many decades before the war. It aroused or unleashed other forces with which the world still was attempting to deal over a half-century later. The war brought about the destruction of some imperial dynasties and virtually an end to the principle of monarchy. It brought about the collapse of some empires and began disintegration of others. It spurred on nationalist movements, aroused popular aspiration for political and social change. The war created conditions which brought to power the Soviet government in Russia and set in motion the world communist movement. It destroyed the European balance of power, drastically weakened European influence in other parts of the world, created many of those conditions which led to the Second World War and its tumultuous aftermath. Had the war never taken place, the world after 1918 would have been a much different place.

For the United States, also, the First World War was an event of momentous importance. It dramatized the nation's coming of age as the world's greatest economic power, and by the end of the war the United States was a major military power as well. When the American president spoke, the world listened, and after 1914 the president found more reason than ever to speak on world affairs. The war showed that national strength can be a two-edged sword. Power to influence world events left the nation responsive to—in some cases at the mercy of—those same world events. Americans who in the twentieth century sometimes brightened with pride in the nation's glory, prestige, and influence found themselves at other times longing for a simple day, when the course of the United States was what the United States had wanted it to be.

The United States played no small part in the war of 1914–18. Even though the nation technically was neutral much of the time—1914–17—its policies as a nonbelligerent had great effect on the duration and direction of the conflict. When the nation did intervene in April 1917, it determined the war's outcome. The timing and circumstances of intervention are important. Had the United States entered the war at another time, under different circumstances, or not at all, the course of the war and, afterward, the course of the world might have been different. This, then, is justification for tracing and interpreting the origins of intervention.

My purpose is to construct a short and, I hope, readable account of the background to American entry into the First World War. Certainly not all information—perhaps even not much of it—in these pages is new, but I do attempt to take into account the most up-to-date archival and secondary research, including my own. While the focus is on the administration of Woodrow Wilson and those domestic forces which influenced its decisions, I also give attention to decision-making in places other than Washington, and particularly to London and Berlin. One might otherwise formulate the false impression that decisions in Washington were the only ones that counted, that the United States was complete master of its fate. As it turned out, persons in Berlin, Paris, and London had a great deal to say about the course of the United States. While I hope that professional historians and specialists in the period will find this volume worthwhile, I have written the book largely for students, on the presumption that understanding where the nation has been in world affairs, and how it got there, might in some small way clarify where it is going.

Several persons and organizations helped in the preparation of this manuscript and deserve my thanks. The Western Michigan University Research Fund provided a grant which facilitated research and writing. The controller of Her Majesty's Stationery Office granted permission to use Crown-copyright papers in the Public Record Office. My student assistants, Earl Peterson and Lynda Ducher, contributed various sorts of assistance along the way. My colleague, John Houdek, read part of the manuscript and offered helpful remarks. James L. Mairs of W. W. Norton & Company gave the manuscript a careful and critical reading, and Elissa Epel did an excellent job of copyediting. A special word of thanks goes to two persons: to Robert H. Ferrell, who read the entire paper and contributed his usual meaningful criticism of style and content; and to my wife, Shirley, who was not only a diligent typist but also a careful editor and encouraging critic.

ROSS GREGORY

Kalamazoo, Michigan

The Origins of
American Intervention in
the First World War

1

The United States and
Its Leaders in 1914

THE CONFLICT which broke out in 1914 was a world war in fact as well as in name. The great battles took place in Europe, but the impact reached much farther, and the war was little less a struggle to dominate the world than to control Europe. The world in 1914 was Europe-centered. Having obtained a head start in the Industrial Revolution, those nations involved in the struggle—Britain, France, Germany, Russia, and Austria-Hungary—held a major portion of the world's economic and military power, with interests far beyond the European continent. When the British lion roared, the sound reached many parts of the world, and so it was with the Russian bear and Prussian tiger. Its empire at a peak, Britain could boast of owning one continent and having colonies in almost every other. Three European nations—Britain, France, and Germany—controlled most of Africa. France and Britain held possessions in North and South America. All the major European powers except Austria-Hungary had colonies or territorial and economic concessions in the Far East. Their governments mostly controlled by monarchies, these regimes behaved the way people expected royalty to act. They held battleship parades, entertained each other in majestic splendor, drew world attention to each movement of kaiser, tsar, or king. Though these performances concealed major problems within, not to mention among, the various states, the European giants did present an impressive picture in 1914. They would have been able to completely dominate world politics except for the rivalry among themselves and the jealous guarding of sectional interests by the governments of Japan and the United States. But these vigorous—or recently invigorated—states had been unable or unwilling to impose their will far beyond spheres of vital concern, and European nations maintained the major voice in the management of the world.

The United States was particularly concerned with the condition of European affairs. That nation had greater association with Europe than many Americans cared to admit, for severance of political ties a century and a half earlier had not meant the end of European influence. The economic relationship was extensive. Most Americans traced their ancestry to one European nation or another; and while there were typically American habits, mores, and attitudes in 1914, in other ways European influence remained strong. Most major intellectual, cultural, and political movements had their origin in Europe. American social and political institutions often represented modification of something found earlier in Britain. The sophisticated man in America liked to stress his foreign connections and tried to imitate Continental ways. Many persons in the United States knew little about European affairs and cared less, but even these individuals unknowingly felt the influence of Europe.

When the World War broke out, however, Americans hastened to stress their differences from Europe. The war was such a dreadful, overwhelming event that it was impossible to grasp what had taken place in Europe or what would come of it. At first glance the conflict seemed a result of highly complicated factors having to do with the same greed and petty jealousy that had plagued Europe for centuries. The United States was above that insanity, the feeling seemed to be, and there quickly developed in the American mind a sense of self-satisfaction, perhaps even superiority, that the United States was spared the turmoil of the Old World. "Now when all this half of the world will suffer the unspeakable brutalization of war," wrote Ambassador Walter Page from London, "we shall preserve our moral strength, our political powers, and our ideals." [1] One conclusion was unmistakably clear: inasmuch as the United States had had no part in the start of the war, it should have no part in its conduct. And with such great distance between the United States and Europe, the nation should have no difficulty going its peaceful way. One observer reflected his countrymen's thoughts when he remarked, "Thank Heaven . . . for . . . the Atlantic Ocean." [2]

What Americans failed to understand was that their position in the war would not depend solely on the nation's geographic isolation. As it turned out, a nation such as Switzerland, resting virtually in the midst of the conflict, found it much less difficult to remain uninvolved than the United States, over three thousand miles from the battlefields. The explanation has to do with a variety of factors: makeup of the population, national economic strength and its relation to world economic affairs, military potential, definition of vital and moral interests. While the geographic position of the United States helped it remain nonbelligerent for several months, in the final analysis it was the nation's world standing that determined its position in the war.

The United States in 1914 was the richest and one of the most powerful nations in the world. It had a population of over ninety million—far larger, if one excludes the colonial empires, than any belligerent save Russia. The years since the Civil War had seen the nation transformed from a predominantly agrarian economy to the world's greatest financial and industrial power, capable of producing a surplus of foodstuffs, machinery, arms, munitions, almost any item useful to nations at war. Americans were not slow to take advantage of this

1. To Woodrow Wilson, Aug. 9, 1914, Burton J. Hendrick, *The Life and Letters of Walter Hines Page* (3 vols., Garden City, N. Y., 1924–26), I, 310–11.
  2. *Ibid.,* 310.

opportunity; they began almost immediately to fill orders from the European belligerents. Years after the war, much sensational attention focused on the war-profiteering of American munitions manufacturers and the bankers who helped finance the traffic. Perhaps these "merchants of death" deserved some of the publicity they received, but it would be a mistake to say they were the only individuals who benefited. The war affected far more American enterprises in addition to dealers in guns and shells. If it fattened dividends paid to stockholders in the Du Pont firm, it also touched the sharecropper in Mississippi and boosted earnings of wheat farmers in Kansas and Nebraska. It was a rare American wage-earner who did not find his income changed by the conflict in Europe.

As a military power the United States in 1914 presented a mixed picture. Because of efforts of such sea-power enthusiasts as Theodore Roosevelt and Captain Alfred T. Mahan, and perhaps even more because of a general world navalist movement, the nation possessed a modern, efficient navy, surpassed in size only by those of Britain and Germany. Although the army, as customary (or as used to be customary) in American history, was not large, more striking than the military forces on hand in 1914 was the national potential. With a huge population and gigantic economic resources, and given the time and will, the United States was capable of military strength superior to that of any nation engaged in the conflict.

The national economic posture made it inevitable that the United States, belligerent or not, would play an important part in the war and find itself deeply affected by the European conflict. The government could take no stand on foreign policy that would not benefit one group of belligerents and harm the other, and every major decision on neutral rights would have an impact on economic conditions in the United States. Paradoxically, growth of American economic strength had in some ways weakened the economy. It had lessened self-sufficiency, made the nation part of a vast international structure which left it vulnerable to change in most parts of the world, particularly if the change occurred in Europe. The outbreak of war did not change the fact that the United States needed to sell products to Europe; neither did it remove American need for materials from European nations and their empires. Of the four nations most involved in commerce with the United States at the start of the war, all were belligerents, three of them major European powers. It often has been argued that with a policy of simple detachment, presumably an embargo on shipments of goods to Europe, the United States could have avoided major problems in the period between 1914 and 1917. But even if such a policy were politically possible—which is by no means certain—it would have created almost endless new difficulty. It would have laid the government and people open to charges of unneutrality, of behavior prejudicial to one group of belligerents and indifferent to moral and legal principles.[3] It also would have invited retaliation from the offended nations and caused major economic problems. It is false to say that the United States could not have survived without its European dealings. The nation had the means to do so. But survival under these conditions would have entailed ability to last out a period of intense economic distress and afterward to rearrange the systems of production and distribution, and perhaps the political system. The United States learned during the war that the merchant needs the customer no less—at least little less—than the customer needs him.

The preceding problems were not apparent to Americans in 1914. Almost unanimous in their desire for neutrality and

3. It is a curious fact that a policy of detachment could be regarded as unneutral and partial. By law and precedent a neutral nation's products were available to any belligerent that could obtain them. In the First World War the Allies easily could obtain American goods, but the Central Powers could not. By imposing an embargo on all shipments to Europe, the United States in fact would have been harming only the Allies. This act would deprive them of goods they desperately needed and felt they had a right to obtain, and deprive the British navy of its most important function. For a discussion of this issue see Arthur S. Link, *Wilson the Diplomatist: A Look at his Major Foreign Policies* (Baltimore, 1957), 35–46.

detachment, they expected commerce with Europe to continue almost as if the war did not exist. Partly, this attitude stemmed from ignorance of what form the war would take or how long it would last. Many thought the war would be over in a few months. There was no way of knowing what a conflict of this magnitude would mean for the United States. No one could remember a similar experience, for the only situation resembling a precedent had existed over a hundred years earlier, during the war between Britain and France at the time of Napoleon, and so much had changed that there seemed little parallel with the war of 1914. Most commentaries written in the United States in August and September viewed the war as an economic opportunity, not the source of great diplomatic complication.

A large group of Americans also exaggerated the nation's ability to have its way in international relations. For over a century—since the War of 1812—the American people had been treated to almost uninterrupted success in foreign affairs. Few persons had stopped to realize that a major explanation for this sparkling record was that the United States had been careful or lucky in choosing its adversaries; that the government had pressed hardest—if necessary, to the point of war— against such weak countries as Spain, Mexico, and the Latin American states, but rarely with major world powers. The two decades before the World War had been a time of much activity beyond continental boundaries. It had taken place without setback, at places of the United States' choosing, and without embroilment in European problems. The American people as a whole (there were exceptions) had not grasped the fact that the nation would find problems as well as benefits in growing up in world affairs. There developed the feeling that success in foreign policy was attributable to military strength or the rightness of American ways. The people assumed that the determinant of American rights and privileges was the United States itself. It is not surprising that Americans became bewildered and angered to discover that belligerent states sought to manipulate the country for their own purposes. All the more frustrating, when both sides were guilty of some violation of American rights, the way to a thorough redressing of grievances offered monumental consequences, perhaps even American intervention.

Neutrality did not mean that the American people failed to develop feelings about the war, although it is difficult to measure what these feelings were. Determination of public opinion is always an imprecise task, even at a time when specialists have perfected sophisticated polling techniques. During the First World War, when there were no polls, interested persons had to resort to less reliable means of measurement, such as editorial opinion in newspapers and contemporary journals; positions taken by well-known and presumably influential individuals; private campaigns on behalf of, or against, some movement; and votes in any election which in a direct or remote way reflected upon the government's wartime policies. Studies show that American opinion varied as to which side it favored and in intensity of feeling. Irish-Americans and German-Americans, together about fifteen percent of the population, were vigorous in opposition to Britain or support of Germany. American Jews, a smaller group, supported the Central Powers, partly because they were of German origin, partly because of anti-Semitism in Russia, a full partner of the Allies. Most of the rest of the population was not pro-German, which means that they were either indifferent, favorable to Britain and France, or hostile to the Central Powers.

Some of the most respected individuals and organs of opinion in the United States were strong supporters of the Allies. Novelists Booth Tarkington and William Dean Howells were in this group, as was former President Theodore Roosevelt. The *New York Times* and *Louisville Courier-Journal* were among the many newspapers. In some measure this attitude was inevitable, a result of long-standing intellectual and economic association between the United States and Great Britain. Then, too, there had been under way for many

years a movement for broader ties with the British. Partly the
movement had its foundation in feelings and theories of race,
for despite the spirit of such revered documents as the Con-
stitution and Declaration of Independence, Americans long had
been willing to note ethnic and racial differences among the
people around them. The tendency to classify peoples always
had characterized the attitude toward the black man in
America; it was manifested in Indian policy, the attitude toward certain immigrants, and finally in the pseudo-scientific
doctrine of Social Darwinism. If, as Social Darwinists had argued, there were superior individuals, it seemed logical to find
superior races; and if American strength somehow was attributable to race, to Anglo-Saxon ancestry, it was difficult to deny
that the British deserved a similar classification. It seemed no
accident that Britain and United States had made great political and economic advancement, and, working together, the
two nations could hasten human progress all over the world.

There were, besides, a few practical-minded persons who
realized that, whatever the rationale for Anglo-American
friendship, British and American interests often coincided,
that the British navy had done much toward enforcing the
Monroe Doctrine. In the late nineteenth century the two nations, for some of the same reasons, had gone on imperialist
binges, and after each state had what it wanted—the United
States its small Pacific empire, Britain over one fourth of the
world—it was anxious to maintain the international *status
quo*. It generally was not a conscious conservatism; few individuals would have argued that the world should stay forever
as it was in 1914. There nonetheless was a popular notion that
countries anxious to seize more territory were acting in a
greedy and dangerous way for orderly civilization. Britain and
the United States then looked with disapproving eye on less
satisfied nations seeking a larger share in the management of
the world. Germany was one of these, for it was, moreover,
arrogant and tactless, and powerful enough to challenge the
leading countries. Indeed, Britain and the United States had

so many forces driving them together that the strong Anglo-Americanism evident in 1914 had come remarkably late.

This is not to say that most persons in the United States supported the movement for Anglo-American *rapprochement*. The group always had been small, but, as mentioned, it included some of the nation's most influential individuals—high officials of government and respected leaders in journalism and education who for years had reminded their listeners of the similarity between British and American principles, institutions, and goals. Starting with such a base in 1914, it was no task at all to portray the European war as a clash between liberty and autocracy, with the Allies fighting to uphold American principles, and their enemies to destroy them. There is no way to measure the full effect of this pro-British group, but it is true that spokesmen for the Allies kept an impressive picture before the American people; and there existed no similarly prestigious group of Americans willing to plead the German case. Anglophilism was one reason why a majority of Americans were, in different degrees of intensity, favorable to the Allies.

Both groups of belligerents made an effort to win American opinion to their side. During 1914 and 1915 the Germans, little less than the British and French, barraged the United States with propaganda. Although it was regarded by some persons as a major factor leading to intervention in 1917, recent studies have questioned if propaganda was important. It is perhaps most accurate to conclude that while propaganda did not—as revisionists have charged—"hoodwink" the American people into a false view of the war, it contributed to an image of the belligerents which had an influence on the general American attitude.[4] In the "battle for image" the Allies, largely the British, won. Britain had the advantage of language, of better lines of communication. It could make good use of such individuals as James Bryce, respected and trusted

4. For a discussion of these authors' views, see Bibliographic Essay, pp. 153–54.

in the United States, and well-known Americans. Allied propaganda efforts concentrated on drawing a similarity between American ideals and reasons for which the Allies were fighting, and in portraying Germany as an unprincipled, savage nation, bent on controlling much of the world.

Much German propaganda was defensive. It was so involved destroying an unfavorable image and creating a favorable one that it could devote little time to discoloring the Allied war effort. Apparently German propaganda did much to weaken the popular feeling that Germany started the war, and that was about its only success. Finally there was the relation between what the belligerents said about their enemies and what the facts seemed to say. The Germans, either tactlessly or as a result of ill fortune, provided periodic inspiration for believing that the British and French were telling the truth, that the Germans were unscrupulous, greedy, barbaric.

The war scarcely had begun when Americans began reading reports about the brutality of German armies in Belgium. A tiny nation with no sizable military power, Belgium had wished to take no part in the conflict, and a treaty signed several decades earlier had pledged the major European powers to respect Belgian neutrality. In defiance of that treaty, the German army had rushed into Belgium as part of a plan to crush France quickly. The Germans were much angered to find the small Belgian army offering resistance, and when civilians took up arms in guerrilla activity, the kaiser's soldiers responded with harsh reprisals. A large number of civilians were executed, and near the end of August the Germans responded to a civilian ambush by totally destroying the city of Louvain. By almost any account German methods in Belgium were vicious and cruel, and the Allies made the most of the situation. American newspapers, ably supplied by British sources, carried almost daily accounts of German atrocities, and in May 1915 Britain issued the Bryce report, a description of pillage, rape, mutilation of bodies—behavior almost unbelievable in a war engaging presumably civilized nations.

"For us the great clear issue of this war is Belgium," wrote the editor of *Life* magazine. "If we see anything right at all in this matter, Belgium is a martyr to civilization, sister to all who love liberty, or law; assailed, polluted, trampled in the mire, heel-marked in her breast, tattered, homeless. . . . The great—unconquerable fact of the great war is Belgium." [5]

Shocked by these and other cruel deeds, the bulk of the American population did see a moral difference between the Allies and their enemies. It would be a mistake, however, to attribute this assessment to stories manufactured by Allied propaganda agencies. The British did manufacture stories, and some Americans probably believed them. But the burning of Louvain was no fabrication, nor was German spy activity in the United States, and there was the sinking of the *Lusitania* in May 1915, an act so shocking as to lead all but the most devout German supporters to question what principles the Germans stood for, if they stood for any. These acts alone were enough to arouse popular indignation, and it is doubtful that opinion would have been very different had Americans been exposed to nothing but truth. The most effective feature of the Allied propaganda campaign was to give broad circulation to the most hideous aspects of German wartime behavior. That these acts seemed justified to the Germans made little difference to Americans long suspicious about values in that land of warriors and *Machtpolitik*.

Even so, one can overemphasize the effect of atrocious German warfare on American neutrality. For some persons the accounts made no difference at all. German-Americans and Irish-Americans remained steadfast in support of the Central Powers. Evidence of German brutality was partly offset by German propaganda, Allied violation of American rights, and the presence of autocratic Russia in the Allied camp. There was, to be sure, frequent criticism of the Germans in American newspapers, but the sharpest attacks came from individu-

5. Cited in Mark Sullivan, *Our Times: The United States, 1900–1925* (6 vols., New York, 1926–35), V. 59.

als already favorable to the Allies. Of those persons who saw a moral difference between the belligerents, few made little movement beyond moral condemnation. Except for a small group of nationalistic activists, Americans did not feel it their nation's responsibility to rid the world of evil forces. The "image" of the Germans eventually helped justify the decision for intervention in 1917, and then affected the way Americans fought the war, but between 1914 and 1917 the American government and people did not allow a vision of German *Schrecklichkeit* to turn them from a position of noninvolvement.

All in all, American opinion remained split during the period of neutrality. A minority was pro-German, other Americans intensely pro-Ally, the bulk of the population somewhere in between, with a majority favorable to Britain and France. Whatever the strength of sympathy for the Allies, the feeling for neutrality was much stronger. Virtually all the people wished to avoid war and expected their government to uphold national honor and neutral rights. The makeup of the population called for the government to take a delicate, often troublesome middle course.

When the World War broke out, the administration of President Woodrow Wilson had been in office nearly a year and a half. The Democrats, controlling the presidency for the first time in sixteen years, had needed this time to refamiliarize themselves with the task of running the national government. During the first few months the administration had been active, gaining major political victories in tariff revision and the Federal Reserve Act. Two other important measures, the Clayton Anti-Trust Bill and Federal Trade Commission Bill, were following the slow path to enactment in Congress. In domestic policy the administration already was well on its way to leaving a mark on American history. In foreign policy the picture was much less clear. The United States faced serious problems in Mexico, a complex situation that in the spring of 1914 almost had brought the two nations to war. The leaders of the administration left the impression that they wished to bring something new to American foreign relations, to help make the world what they thought it should be; but it was difficult to know what the Wilsonians had in mind.

Any discussion of foreign policy during the Wilson years is conspicuous in the attention given President Wilson. This attention is justified, for during the World War of 1914–18 the president, more than at any period before and perhaps any period since, made foreign policy. While there was a sound constitutional basis for presidential leadership in foreign affairs, the state of the government in 1914–18 had much to do with the background and personality of Wilson. Few scholars will accept the unflattering psychoanalytic treatment accorded Wilson in the posthumous book by Sigmund Freud and William C. Bullitt published in 1967, but no student will deny that Wilson was a remarkably complex individual. Of southern birth and upbringing, he never ceased to feel the influence of his surroundings. At home he had been exposed to strong patriarchal leadership, saturated with Presbyterian theology (his father was a minister), repeatedly reminded of sharp differences between good and evil, of the necessity of discovering and carrying out God's plan. Wilson was not an easy man to know, his friendship difficult to keep. Effective and often inspiring before large groups of people, he had difficulty with person-to-person relations. Associates found him uncomfortable, cold and aloof, unwilling to treat them as equals. A person with rigid standards often will find himself isolated, but in Wilson's case it seemed much a matter of choice. He apparently did not want close friends. The single exception, beyond his wife, was Colonel Edward M. House, and in final analysis perhaps House was no exception after all: House did manage a close relationship for some years, between 1911 and 1919, but when the two men came to serious disagreement over the Treaty of Versailles, Wilson would have no more to do with his former comrade, would not see him again, even though Wilson lived on for several years thereafter, until 1924, ensconced in a lonely house on "S" Street in Washington.

Wilson's profession, once he found it, was peculiarly suited to fostering these personality tendencies. Unsuccessful at law, he obtained a Ph.D. in political science at Johns Hopkins and settled on a career in teaching and scholarly publication, eventually rising to a professorship and then to the presidency of Princeton. In the classroom he was—as professors are wont to be—the expositor of truth. He obtained a reputation as an inspiring lecturer but was not as effective dealing with individual students. As president he regarded the university as his fief and treated challenges to his supremacy as a personal affront. Anyone who dealt with the ascetic, hard-jawed Presbyterian with the straight mouth and the unblinking eyes knew he was facing a man of determination. More than one unhappy associate accused him—but not to his face—of thinking he was Jesus Christ. He did not yield gracefully. Indeed, as is well-known, Wilson's entry into politics came partly as a result of unwillingness to live with defeat in a struggle for administrative power with a dean at Princeton.

Once president of the United States and compelled to treat foreign problems, these same traits shone through. Wilson exercised a leadership even more striking than in domestic affairs. During the period of neutrality he kept a close watch on almost all aspects of policy and wrote many diplomatic dispatches himself. No less than in personal matters, he sought ways to do God's bidding (at least what he saw as God's bidding) so as to place the conduct of foreign relations on a high moral plane. Hence Wilsonian diplomacy has become, to advocates of so-called realist diplomacy (an unemotional, practical approach which stresses national interest), synonymous with idealism and moralism.

Much has been made of Wilson's coming to the presidency ignorant of foreign affairs. Few accounts of the period fail to cite the Wilsonian remark to a friend: "It would be the irony of fate if my administration had to deal chiefly with foreign affairs." It is true that his academic writings had focused on domestic problems and the workings of the American government; his five-volume history of the United States had passed hurriedly over dealings with foreign nations. But it does not necessarily follow that different academic preparation would have changed the way he handled foreign policy. He was so concerned with principle, so convinced that nations no less than men must act for high purposes of humanity, that more study of international affairs likely would have confirmed what he thought true: that traditional state behavior based on balances of power and national selfishness had brought nothing but distrust, rumors of war, and now in 1914 the great conflict. It is important to note that Wilson, when he led the nation to war in April 1917, had had four years of experience as leader in foreign relations and almost three years to study the European situation. From this point the president moved not to cold-hearted practicality but to greater idealism, not to adjust to the old system and restore what could be salvaged, but to devise a new structure for interstate relations.

How did these personality characteristics make themselves felt in diplomacy of the Wilson years? On the positive side they provided direction, a strength of presidential leadership that weaker, less determined men could not provide. Wilson won some diplomatic victories out of sheer persistence and dedication to purpose. Few individuals could match him as an articulator of national and human goals. He admonished men to look beyond themselves to a better world, guided by Christian brotherhood, immune from the petty bickering of the past. For those who followed, it was an exciting quest, the goals well worth seeking.

For those who resisted, it seemed a foolish venture. Opponents often thought Wilson thoroughly visionary, out of touch with reality. Leaders of foreign governments scoffed at his idealism and resented his efforts to impose his thoughts on other nations. Convinced he was right, Wilson frequently saw as wrong the proposals of other persons, giving the impression of infallibility and superiority of intellect and understanding. Opponents who found this stiffening manner distasteful resisted what proposals Wilson offered, perhaps because they thought them wrong, perhaps because Wilson proposed them.

Of course this assessment—indeed any assessment of Wilson—bears the danger of overstatement and simplification. Wilson was so exceptionally complex that anyone describing him is tempted to carry generalization too far. His traits of character and behavior were not absolute. He did not make all the decisions in foreign policy. Not insensitive to feeling of his secretaries of state, he occasionally allowed them to pursue separate policies. Ignorance sometimes left him compelled to ask for guidance. While it might be possible to generalize about Wilsonian diplomacy as a whole, some policies fitted the mold better than others. Wilson was noted for inflexibility, but some of the sharpest criticism occurred as a result of his compromises at Paris in 1919. Even though he did make the important decisions during the period of neutrality, he did not make the problems; the problems did much to fashion the response. He had to deal with the world as he found it and not as what he would have liked it to be. Policy often was no more than a choice between alternatives placed before him by the course of the United States and the belligerent nations. He did set high moral standards for himself and his nation, but it is unsafe to assume that his policies were in all respects unrealistic and impractical. Moralism and realism do not automatically clash. Moral policy, depending upon what one interprets moralism to mean, might be in the nation's best interests.

Of Wilson's advisers in foreign policy the most important bore no title other than that of friend. Edward M. House of Texas—commonly called Colonel House, even though he was no military man—could have had almost any government post, but he preferred to work the fringes and by these means be of service to his friend in the White House, while enjoying remarkable power and prestige. House clearly was Wilson's intimate friend and confidant. "Mr. House is my second personality," the president once said. "He is my independent self. His thoughts and mine are one. If any one thinks he is reflecting my opinion by whatever action he takes, they are welcome to the conclusion." [6] Even so, it is possible to overstate House's importance. He obtained his position largely by fostering, and not attempting to change, Wilson's most striking habits of mind and character. Once Wilson's mind was set, House was no more successful than anyone else in changing it, and so he rarely tried. He often advised the president along lines to which he felt Wilson already was inclined. One associate disdainfully called the Colonel "as timid a dependent-in-thought as one man ever found in another," which might be an overstatement, but not by much.[7] An independent course might have provided the president new advice. It likely also would have ended House's privileged position.

House was in some ways helpful, in other ways harmful to the president. His friendship was a source of comfort to a man prone to loneliness; his quiet conversation often helped Wilson sort out his thoughts. Now and then House inspired steps the president was willing to follow. The Colonel's trips to Europe in 1915 and 1916 to seek out belligerent feeling about presidential mediation were House's idea, and although they did not succeed, he did establish shorter, less formal lines of communication between the administration and belligerent governments. At times the Colonel's behavior became troublesome. The ambassador in London became so disturbed at what he regarded a usurpation of his responsibilities that he was prepared to resign if House continued meddling in affairs abroad. House could not fail to be impressed with his ability to speak for the American government. Subservient in Wilson's presence, he was not always cautious away from the president. On extended journeys the Colonel sometimes became separated from the full intent of his government and, interjecting personal thoughts, occasionally made his govern-

6. Charles Seymour, ed., *The Intimate Papers of Colonel House* (4 vols., Boston, 1926–28), I, 114.

7. The Diary of Walter Hines Page, April 1, 1917, Houghton Library, Harvard University.

ment appear many-sided, bewildering, and misleading.

Scholars often have held up House as possessing a realistic view of diplomacy, which meant that while he wished an Allied victory and earlier American intervention, he did not want Germany so weakened as to destroy the balance of European power. If such was the gist of House's diplomacy, it was a failure, for somewhere along the line the idea of a balanced peace was lost. But House, for reasons no less emotional than practical, developed a favoritism for the Allies and was willing earlier than Wilson to have the United States enter the conflict. Ever so quietly and tactfully he kept before the president the idea that, whatever happened, the United States must not press Britain and France too hard. If any person influenced Wilson along these lines, it was House.

Whatever House's effect on American diplomacy, he was in one way of undeniable great importance. Blessed with financial security, he kept a secretary with him almost all the time. He dictated full diaries of each day's events and kept up a lively correspondence with many American and world leaders. The "House papers"—four volumes were published after the war—quickly became, and remain, an amazing depository of information on Wilson and the Wilson administration.

Wilson's first secretary of state was by most standards a poor choice. The appointment of William Jennings Bryan to that high post reflected an unfortunate but not fully avoidable feature of American politics. Bryan's selection came as result of his standing in the Democratic Party and his influence with Democrats in Congress, not because of any grounding in foreign affairs. A native of the Great Plains, Bryan had focused his activity and thought on a few themes: the problems of agricultural America, furtherance of fundamentalist Protestant ideals, the interests of the Democratic Party. Bryan had almost no preparation in foreign affairs, and his brief tenure as secretary of state did little to add perception to his outlook.

The Democratic presidential candidate in three elections, he was a remarkable figure. Big, even robust, a hearty eater, indeed a consumer of whole fried chickens (he could eat two or three at a sitting), he could shout his speeches for a distance of several city blocks and enthralled Americans of the pre-loudspeaker age who came to see but, especially, to hear. He was a man of towering vitality. Long years on the campaign trail had produced many friends, enemies, and sharply differing opinions of his talents. To followers he was a hero, and leader, an example of what had been scarce in American politics: an honest public servant, devoted to the needs of the common man. He had convinced his supporters of the need to strip away ritual and pretense and make the American government a simple, direct servant of the masses. Critics found Bryan impractical, out of step with the world, perhaps a hypocrite. He spoke so much of religion that opponents, somewhat ungenerously, would allow him no human shortcoming, and they were willing to exploit the slightest opportunity for criticism or ridicule. They questioned whether a man of principle could function at the same time as semi-evangelist and Democrat stalwart. Noticeably balding, he wore what hair was left, long in the back, dressed in long waistcoats at a time when such fashions were out of style. For a man pledged to temperance he seemed to have an intemperate appetite. For a man whose God was not money he seemed to have a remarkable attraction to the funds he could acquire from private speaking engagements. While secretary of state he insisted upon lecturing to Chautauqua audiences where, in some persons' judgment, he degraded his high office by appearing in the company of jugglers, Swiss yodelers, or other undignified acts. Subject to almost perpetual harassment from the Eastern press, he was considered, by many, unfit for his post.

Bryan fared only slightly better with officials of the American and foreign governments. Wilson always treated him kindly; he considered Bryan honest and sincere, but of limited intellectual capability, and if important foreign problems came up the president took personal charge. Lesser officials who spoke to Bryan with respect were often unkind outside his presence. Foreign diplomats found him visionary, unsophisticated, and rigid in his beliefs. "Mr. Bryan is, I should think," wrote the British ambassador, Sir Cecil Spring-Rice, "unlike any other Secretary of State or Minister for Foreign Affairs that has ever been known. He regards the matter simply from the politician's point of view." [8] Bryan's reputation did not enhance the chances for policy he wished to promote.

Like his chief in the White House, Bryan saw it as America's world mission to advance right-doing and Christian principles among nations. Foremost among these ideals was the preservation of peace. "Bryan spoke to me of peace as he always does," wrote Spring-Rice another time. "He sighs for the Nobel Prize and besides that he is a really convinced peaceman. He has just given me a sword beaten into a ploughshare six inches long to serve as a paperweight. It is adorned with quotations from Isaiah and himself." [9] Before the war Bryan sought to preserve peace through a series of "cooling-off" treaties, the signers of which, in face of crisis, would agree to wait twelve months before starting hostilities. Although the secretary negotiated such treaties with thirty nations, neither he nor anyone else invoked any of them. After the war began Bryan had two goals: to keep the United States out of the conflict at almost any cost, and to use the government's offices to bring the war in Europe to a halt. Wilson did not allow Bryan much liberty to pursue the latter object. He thought the secretary's timing was not right and came to believe reports about Bryan's low standing with European governments. Any initiative by the secretary of state, he feared, would weaken his own efforts to promote peace in Europe. Pursuance of the first goal led to Bryan's resignation during the *Lusitania* crisis with Germany, in June 1915, at which time he argued that it was

8. Ambassador Sir Cecil Spring-Rice to Sir Edward Grey, March 2, 1914, The Papers of Sir Edward Grey, Public Record Office, London.
9. To Sir Arthur Nicolson, Nov. 13, 1914, Stephen Gwynn, ed., *The Letters and Friendships of Sir Cecil Spring-Rice* (2 vols., London, 1929), II, 240.

better to yield some alleged neutral rights than face the danger of war.

Most scholars agree that Bryan's proposals, though sincere and courageously expressed, were unworkable. Their strength rests upon answers to two major questions of the period of neutrality: Could the United States survive in a satisfactory manner detached from Europe if it came to that point? Did it matter to the United States who won the war, or whether the war should have a winner? Perhaps the most striking feature of Bryan's secretaryship was the slight thought he gave such questions. Bryan's large voice could not be ignored, and his followers needed to be represented in the Wilson administration, but the State Department was not the place for the Great Commoner. The most neutral of all Wilson's advisers, he in final analysis had little effect. He probably exerted greater influence outside the government, where he gave expression to the pacifist views of his followers, not a small group. While Wilson never came to agree with this group, its presence balanced the advocates of intervention and helped convince him that a middle course was best.

Like his predecessor, Robert Lansing became secretary of state more as a result of circumstances than because of his talents. Wilson told House he chose Lansing as Bryan's successor because he "would not be troublesome by obtruding or injecting his own views," a statement in full conformity with the president's intent of managing foreign relations himself.[10] This is not to say that Lansing held no impressive credentials, for he was well educated and experienced in international law and diplomacy. His father-in-law, John W. Foster, had been secretary of state in the administration of Benjamin Harrison. More important was the fact that Lansing was in the right place at the right time. As counselor of the State Department, he had been Bryan's second in command and had handled much of the Department's work in relations with European

10. House Diary, July 24, 1915, The Diary and Papers of Edward M. House, Yale University Library.

belligerents. The appointment was a convenient decision which aroused no controversy in the American press or major capitals and, as Wilson surmised, allowed the president to go his way with a minimum of internal friction.

Lansing's manner of diplomacy does not lend itself to simple generalization. Assuming in 1914 that neutrality was the proper course for the United States, he then had tended to view policy in terms of international law. Some time in 1915 he became convinced that German defeat was essential for the United States; he was prepared long before the president to have his nation enter the conflict. It is not difficult to find evidence to suggest that despite his legalist inclinations Lansing was at heart a realist who gave due respect to force and recognized the difficulty of defining good and evil in international relations. "Lansing exhibited . . . [a] curious state of mind," House's diary noted in 1915. "He believes that almost any form of atrocity is permissible provided a nation's safety is involved." [11] Lansing came to feel that submarine warfare was a threat to American interests, not the least of which was the economic consideration, and while there is no evidence that he feared Germany eventually would attack the United States, he concluded that a German victory in Europe would be contrary to America's future well-being. At the same time the secretary, at least in private memoranda, yielded to moral judgments of his own. His pro-Ally and anti-German feeling stemmed partly from the fact that he regarded the German government as undemocratic, immoral, and an evil world force.

In relations with Wilson, Lansing did as well as he could, considering the president's temperament. Wilson made the major decisions, and if Lansing disagreed he was careful not to press too hard. As counselor of the Department he had given the president legal advice which in the first months of war was helpful in laying the basis for neutrality policy. Despite his conviction that the Allies must win the war, he favored keep-

11. *Ibid.*

ing steady pressure on the British and French. On the surface there appeared, with rare exceptions, a picture of harmony—the president and loyal secretary of state. Lansing always looked proper in public. He was handsome, adorned with well-groomed mustache and hair, smartly dressed, dignified, restrained; he usually avoided saying or doing anything controversial—the sort of man one might expect Wilson to have as secretary of state. Beneath the surface there was less harmony than the public or even the president knew. Though Lansing never engaged in bitter argument with his chief, he did come to disagree with some of Wilson's policies and occasionally moved to weaken their force. The purpose of these maneuvers, and, indeed, of much of Lansing's diplomacy, was to avoid action harmful to the British and French. Inasmuch as these nations steered clear of American reprisal, and the United States eventually joined the war against Germany, one can conclude that Lansing accomplished his major objectives. He was not the dominant force in foreign policy but made his presence felt. He had knowledge in areas where the president was weak, maintained good relations with House, and dealt with Wilson cautiously enough to keep his job.

Other persons in the State Department and Diplomatic Service brought to their posts sharply differing amounts of experience and competence. Frank L. Polk, who became counselor in 1915, took an active part in policy, sometimes filling in for the secretary of state. He impressed many as being a more capable man than Lansing. Other individuals who had a hand in department policy included House's young friend William Phillips, Solicitor Cone Johnson, James Brown Scott of the government's neutrality board, and Chandler P. Anderson, who became a special legal adviser. All these individuals were competent in their areas; with the possible exception of Johnson, all were favorable to the Allies. Persons sent to diplomatic stations abroad were for the most part individuals with few qualifications to hold the post. Walter Hines Page, the ambassador to Great Britain, was the most interesting of the lot. Page had no training in diplomacy and little grounding in foreign policy, but he was intelligent, articulate, and could turn his talents in many directions. A friend of Wilson, for a while he had the president's ear. The problem with Page was that he saw his task as, largely, to foster friendship with the British. He liked the role so well and was so successful that he wanted to do nothing else. He became so intensely pro-British and antagonistic to American efforts to preserve neutrality that he fell from grace in Washington, thus wasting his extraordinary talents. Most other ambassadorial assignments went for the purpose of paying political debts or finding persons able to bear expenses of major foreign posts. So it was with James W. Gerard, who became ambassador to Germany; William G. Sharp, ambassador to France; and Thomas Nelson Page, ambassador to Italy. Bryan had a major part in the appointment of ministers (diplomatic agents of the second rank), and there followed an almost disgraceful disregard for competence and professionalism in favor of appointment on the basis of friendship and party loyalty.

All in all one might say that the Wilson administration was fashioned after the nineteenth century. It placed an overwhelming emphasis on problems at home. American stations abroad suffered from lack of funds and suitable places of business. Ambassadorial and ministerial appointments came out of the patronage hopper. In appointing Bryan the president even sacrificed the secretaryship of state to bolster chances of a successful domestic policy. In these respects the administration was similar to most preceding administrations, except perhaps the presidency of Theodore Roosevelt. The Wilson administration was dissimilar in that it had Wilson at its head.

One final point needs to be made about the individuals charged with helping manage American foreign policy. Wilson, as mentioned, did not rely on them as much as they sometimes felt he should. He did much of the work himself or relied on independent contacts, usually House. The president's manner and his stubbornness of mind fostered suspicion within subordinate officials, and the administration suffered from more than the normal amount of disloyalty and men working at cross purposes. Page, in collaboration with British officials in London, later received the most publicity for this sort of behavior. Lansing was guilty of serious efforts to undermine the president. Even Colonel House occasionally tried to guide policy contrary to the president's wishes. Of course, Wilson's advisers did not broadcast their activity; much of it was never known to the president and did not become public knowledge until years after the war when the private papers and government documentary collections were opened for research and examination.

In view of the preceding observations, it is perhaps surprising that the administration fared as well as it did in foreign relations. There were problems of policy and personnel. Officials sometimes tampered with policy in ways they should not have. Bryan resigned not long after the war started, and Wilson came close to dismissing Lansing and replacing Page. Despite these troubles the American ship of state sailed on, if at times unsteadily. This fact suggests that in the Wilson administration men other than the president had but slight opportunity to guide policy. They might cause some off-course sailing, but never a permanent change in direction. It suggests as well that the United States at times was in the grasp of forces larger than even the will of the president.

The First World War broke out in the last days of July and the first part of August 1914. With public officials what they were in 1914, and with American opinion inclined to view policy in terms of the noninterventionist tradition, the government could do little more than follow a short-range, step-by-step approach to the war, treating problems as they occurred.

2

Establishment of
Benevolent Neutrality

〰〰〰〰〰〰〰〰〰〰〰〰〰〰〰〰〰〰〰〰〰〰〰〰〰〰

AMERICANS who first felt the influence of the World War were not soldiers, shippers, or government officials but ordinary citizens who happened to be traveling in Europe when the shooting started. They had come for various reasons, business perhaps; a good many were there to partake of European beauty and culture, such quaint places as the cafés on the Champs Elysées, Westminster Abbey, or Vienna with its nineteenth-century grace and charm. Prepared to see the best features of European civilization, they now had to face some of the Old Continent's worst. The war started with remarkable speed, and to say that these people experienced bewilderment, worry, and shock would be a great understatement. Even though propaganda mills immediately began to turn out stories of how the conflict had started, these marooned Americans—there were perhaps sixty thousand of them—were less concerned about the war's causes than how it would affect them. They hoped it would not affect them at all. They only wished to get home. Perhaps the most moving description of the scene came from Ambassador Page in London, one of those responsible for arranging the American departure: "Crazy men and weeping women were imploring and cursing and demanding —God knows it was bedlam turned loose. I have been called a man of the greatest genius for an emergency by some, by others a damned fool, by others every epithet between these extremes. Men shook English banknotes in my face and demanded United States money and swore our Government and its agent ought all to be shot. Women expected me to hand them steamship tickets home. . . . Yesterday one poor American woman yielded to the excitement and cut her throat. . . . People stop me on the street, follow me to luncheon, grab me as I come out of any committee meeting— to know my opinion of this or that—how can they get home? . . . I have not had a bath for three days: as soon as I got in the tub, the telephone rang an 'urgent' call!" [1]

Americans in Europe had problems people in the United States did not face, but in one important way their reaction reflected an almost unanimous American judgment of the conflict: the war was a foreign affair which should be left to the Europeans. It is not surprising that the first sounding of American policy from the initial hectic days reflected an intention to keep the war at a distance. Emotional and uncomplicated, it carried the message that America's major object was to stand off and treat belligerents equally. Wilson proclaimed neutrality and appealed for Americans to remain neutral in thought. He refused to authorize the sale of dismantled submarines to Britain, acquiesced in Bryan's desire for a ban on loans to nations at war, allowed the State Department to seek approval of a broad range of neutral rights. Deluged from the beginning with reports of atrocious warfare, Wilson refused to say anything and then announced in September that he would not take a stand.

These first pronouncements, on the surface so safe and purely neutral, were to become the object of a considerable controversy in later years. Some historians, who fully approved the moves, have pointed to the first weeks of war as the only period of American neutrality. By changing some of the policy, they have argued, the administration changed as well its neutral posture and desire to maintain detachment. Plausible as that argument might seem, it overlooks some important factors. In large measure the first American response to the

1. To Woodrow Wilson, Aug. 9, 1914, Hendrick, *Page,* I, 304–5, 308, 309.

war reflected innocence—ignorance of what the war would mean for the United States. Wilson did not know much about these matters to begin with, and in the first days he did little to educate himself. He still gave close attention to domestic measures before Congress, and to his wife's serious illness. Her death on August 6, the day after Britain declared war on Germany, moved him to deepest distress. He allowed Bryan to sponsor the ban on loans and approved the State Department's effort to have a rigidly structured document, the Declaration of London of 1909, accepted by all belligerents as a code of neutral rights.[2] It soon became evident that a policy of simple detachment was impractical, unworkable, not suited to the needs of the United States. Offered in a spirit of impartiality, the first statements of policy if put in effect would have had a partial and perhaps an unneutral result. Their introduction reflected differences between the ideal and the real, how the United States might have stood had it been untouched by major world events.

In weeks to come the administration modified some of the positions taken in the first days of war. Statements involving mere expression of intent, requiring no practical application, stood as they were. Wilson of course did not withdraw his proclamation of neutrality, that is, not until April 1917; and not until that time did he lose his desire to stay out of the war. He had to redefine what neutrality meant. He did not abandon the request for neutrality in thought, although it soon became evident that few people, not even the president, could adhere to that high standard. He maintained his silence on the atrocity stories. The president and State Department did make important changes pertaining to loans and neutral rights. Before

2. The Declaration of London represented the most recent effort to codify neutral rights. Drawn up in 1909 by a conference that included American representatives, it was not international law in 1914 because participating governments had not ratified it. As will be seen, the document placed restrictions on contraband—goods subject to seizure by belligerent navies. Because of this and other provisions, it was highly beneficial to neutral nations wishing to engage in wartime commerce.

the end of 1914 the Department with Wilson's approval had allowed American financial firms to provide credit for belligerent countries. By 1917 it was possible to float loans of many millions of dollars in the United States. Almost all the loans and credit went to the British and French. Before the start of 1915 the American government had abandoned its insistence on the principles of the Declaration of London and showed an inclination to accept a British interpretation of neutral rights. The American definition of neutrality generally changed from efforts toward impartiality and equal treatment to the practice of dealing with belligerents in accord with problems faced with each nation. The problems with each nation were different, and so treatment also differed. These changes came to be part of an economic link between the Allies and the United States, the importance of which is almost impossible to exaggerate. For the Allies it came to be the difference between life and death, for the United States, at least, between prosperity and depression.

The economic enmeshment of the United States developed in a step-by-step process and not as a result of deliberate design. It began as a means of promoting American economic interests, of upholding neutral rights, and not suiting the purposes of any belligerent. Individuals inside and outside of government felt it right and necessary that the United States continue to trade with Europe and saw no reason why commercial relations should be detrimental to neutrality. The first weeks of war were highly uncertain. The United States beforehand had been in an economic decline which the conflict threatened to make worse. Faced with heavy unloading of English securities, the stock market skidded and then closed. With all European markets disrupted, the price of cotton dropped sharply; by August 1914 cotton was worth half the price obtainable in July. Southern states faced the prospect of a severe depression, and other parts of the nation stood to suffer economic loss unless foreign markets soon righted themselves. Even though some people, Secretary of the Treasury William Gibbs McAdoo included, saw the conflict as a means of enriching the United States, the concern in the first weeks of war was with keeping what trade the nation had.

The administration took action to help. To bolster the tiny American merchant fleet, it pushed through Congress a bill which allowed American-owned ships of foreign registry to be reregistered under the American flag, and looked for other ways to assist the acquisition of new vessels. It introduced another measure designed to permit the government to begin purchase of ships. After a long controversy, the measure failed to pass. The administration gave formal sanction to sale of goods to Europe, including contraband, and, as mentioned, sought a clear understanding of American neutral rights. Thus Wilson and his advisers set out to press for two major American objects: maintenance of trade with Europe and preservation of neutrality, not fully conscious that these paths were not fully reconcilable, that action to promote one would jeopardize the other.

The initial problems of neutrality grew out of efforts to promote a large trade with the European belligerents. Inasmuch as the United States expected the belligerents to behave according to the rules of maritime warfare, it had to operate within its limits. International law allowed rights for combatants as well as neutral nations in time of war. The administration was willing to allow trade with all nations at war, but the nations had to be in a position to obtain it. The dominant factor in neutral trading during the First World War, as events soon revealed, was Britain's control of the sea, which meant that the Allies could obtain most of the American supplies they wanted, and while Germany and Austria-Hungary needed fewer American goods, these nations found it difficult to obtain any products at all. By the autumn of 1914 the Royal Navy had swept the German merchant marine from the sea. The only way Germany could receive American supplies was in neutral vessels—American, or those of some other nonbelligerent nation—and even in these circumstances the British could claim certain rights under international law. They could intercept goods defined as absolute contraband, items of war.

Neutral nations understood this fact and did not attempt to ship directly to the Central Powers goods commonly accepted as contraband.[3] The British also could seize conditional contraband—goods clearly destined for the military forces (and not civil population) of the enemy. They could seize any goods at all in places where they could impose an effective and legal blockade. Although they never formally proclaimed a blockade, the British often acted as if they had. Since there was no official blockade, neutral nations theoretically were free to ship to belligerent states all items not classified as absolute contraband and not proven conditional contraband. They presumably were free to trade among themselves in any goods they chose. While before 1914 virtually all nations had given formal approval to these general principles of international law, great problems arose in attempting to apply the rules. Material useful in warfare changed with the perfection of new military techniques, and there existed no international commission to keep rules up to date. Neutral nations wanted a small number of items classified as contraband; belligerents with large navies wanted long contraband lists. It was difficult to prove that an item was or was not conditional contraband. Problems arose in areas where international law was silent or outmoded, or where there were differences in interpretation. Under ideal conditions the United States could have enjoyed a lively trade with the Central Powers and with continental nations not involved in the conflict. As it turned out, traffic with Central Europe virtually came to a halt.

Before this situation came to exist, the Wilson administration made a sustained attempt at obtaining legal sanction for a broad range of neutral rights. The war was but a few days old when the State Department dispatched to belligerents a suggestion that they abide by the Declaration of London of 1909. Had the powers accepted this document, the United States

3. They did, however, attempt to disguise contraband goods and slip them by the British navy. On one occasion a shipment of onions was found to be rubber when one of the "onions," dropped on the deck, bounced high in the air. British officials were not amused by this practice, and it inspired them to be deliberate in inspecting neutral ships.

would have had a clear definition of rights and a series of maritime liberties seldom experienced in time of war. The Declaration included a small category of contraband items and a long list of goods classified as "free" which never could be made contraband.

The major problem was that the United States could not invoke the Declaration as the law of nations, because the governments had not yet ratified what the international commission had proposed. The British Parliament, ever suspicious of any agreement that tampered with sea power, expressly had rejected it. The United States could only ask that the nations accept it as binding during the World War. The Central Powers were happy to comply. Austria-Hungary had no naval strength to speak of, and the German navy, though large, was not strong enough to contain the British fleet. Germany in 1914 based its hope for victory on a large, efficient land-military machine. Willing to accept rules which would impose a general limit on sea power, the Central Powers accepted the Declaration of London on condition that their enemies did. Of course the Allies had a far different view, for they did not wish to accept rules that would limit using British naval supremacy to prevent supplies from reaching the enemy. The British government accepted the Declaration only by retaining the right to change certain parts of it. The State Department let the matter drop for well over a month, then, faced with steadily tightening British restriction, it resurrected the Declaration in late September 1914.

The dispute which followed is important in several respects. The first major controversy for the United States during the war, it gave the British and American governments an idea of what each expected of the other and what barriers stood in the way of peaceful wartime relations between the two English-speaking states. Officially the United States dealt with all the major Allies, but inasmuch as most of the problems involved matters of trade, and inasmuch as the British, with its sea power, determined Allied naval policy, the disputes were largely between Britain and the United States. The subsequent settlement did not remove all outstanding issues, but it suggested that other problems might be treated in similar manner. The tone of discussion was friendly throughout, and while neither nation wished to yield major points, both sides sought to reach an agreement that produced the least possible inconvenience or ill-feeling. In short, the discussion showed that in relations with the United States, Britain had an advantage that its enemies did not have.

The dispute also brought to the fore and illuminated the attitude of the men responsible for wartime diplomacy. On the American side, President Wilson, though certainly influential, was not yet the force he soon would become. Wilson supervised the general course of policy; now and then he changed dispatches to make them diplomatically palatable. He often approved what the State Department placed before him. While House occasionally interjected an opinion, he played no important part in the discussion over the Declaration of London. Bryan, for one reason or another—usually to campaign for the elections of 1914—was absent from Washington much of the time, leaving Counselor Lansing to set much of the tone and content of policy. Not yet convinced of the wisdom of American intervention, or even of German defeat, Lansing pressed for a full expression of American neutral rights, the basis for which he hoped to find in the Declaration of London. Having the lawyer's flair for technicality and not the president's flair for words, he sometimes sent messages sounding more harsh than he intended. In Washington Lansing dealt most with Ambassador Spring-Rice. The latter envoy, although he came to earn in Washington and London a reputation for excitability and irascibility, kept calm during the discussion over the Declaration of London and was a competent spokesman for his government.

In London the key figure was the foreign secretary, Sir Edward Grey. Wise and experienced in the ways of diplomacy, he was ideally suited to influence Americans with whom he had to deal. He did not fit the American image of the arrogant, self-seeking, only slightly believable European diplomat.

Quiet and serious, sad-faced, almost mournful, with friendly eyes and upright, clean-shaven countenance, he carried a burden most of the time, fashioned by worries of war and from fear of damage the United States could inflict on the Allied war effort. War was not his forte, he told American friends. He would rather study birds or English literature, or go fishing. He performed his warlike tasks only to prevent barbarians from overrunning the world. What American could quarrel with such objectives? The American ambassador described Grey as Lincolnesque and other supremely flattering terms; House regarded him an intimate friend. Even Wilson from a distance admired the foreign secretary's peaceful, sincere manner.

Though Grey was not as open and frank as he led American associates to believe, his behavior was by no means all pretension. He was a thoughtful, cultivated man who felt some sympathy for American wishes to renovate diplomacy along lines of honesty and mutual trust. He was, above all, sincere in his freely expressed desire to promote American friendship, a goal he had regarded since coming to office in 1905 as a "cardinal principle" of British diplomacy. In his memoirs published in the mid-1920s he set down what he had considered the major problem of foreign policy during the World War: "blockade of Germany was essential to the victory of the Allies, but the ill-will of the United States meant their certain defeat. . . . The allies soon became dependent for an adequate supply on the United States. If we quarrelled with the United States we could not get that supply. It was better therefore to carry on the war without blockade, if need be, than to incur a break with the United States about contraband and thereby deprive the Allies of the resources necessary to carry on the war at all or with any chance of success. The object of diplomacy . . . was to secure the maximum of blockade that could be enforced without a rupture with the United States." [4] While Grey wrote these words years after

4. Viscount Grey of Fallodon (Sir Edward Grey), *Twenty-five Years, 1892–1916* (2 vols., New York, 1925), II, 107.

the conflict had ended, documents show that he felt exactly the same way during his time in office. They show also that he experienced considerable difficulty finding a "safe maximum" of blockade. The Foreign Office had its "ginger" group which believed Grey lenient in dealings with the United States; almost all advisers—Arthur Nicolson, Sir Eyre Crowe, Lord Robert Cecil—urged a harder British line. So, intermittently, did important newspapers, and the French and Russian allies. Grey nonetheless persisted along a cautious course and more often than not was able to prevail.

If Grey seemed to his colleagues a bit too gentle, he was to American diplomats a thoroughly honest and decent fellow. Indeed, those Americans who dealt with him behaved almost as if he acted to uphold American interests and not simply to find workable British foreign policy. Such certainly was the case with Ambassador Page. Pro-British on arrival in London in 1913, Page allowed himself to be caught up by the prospect of Anglo-American friendship, an ideal he felt the foreign secretary shared. If the English-speaking nations would cooperate, he foresaw them leading a new world era of democracy and economic betterment. Page thought that the World War, dreadful as it seemed, might be a blessing, for it could hasten Anglo-American cooperation and destroy German militarism. After a few sessions with Grey, he was willing to accept the British view of the war and what responsibilities that view carried. "If German bureaucratic brute force could conquer Europe," he wrote House, "presently it would try to conquer the United States; and we should all go back to the era of war as man's chief industry and back to the domination of kings by divine right. It seems to me, therefore, that the Hohenzollern idea must perish—be utterly strangled in the making of peace." [5] Page came to the conclusion that his nation should not bother Britain with technical aspects of neutral rights, and that the United States should yield in all important cases involving British curtailment of American trade with Germany. It seemed a small American contribution to the battle for lib-

5. Sept. 22, 1914, Hendrick, *Page,* I, 327–28.

erty and democracy. The continuing willingness of the State
Department to press the Declaration of London drove him to
deep distress. He experienced sleepless nights, became angry
on reading his government's dispatches, threatened to resign,
and finally joined forces with Grey to seek a way to circum-
vent the American position. The controversy over the Declaration of London began a period of strained relations
between Washington and the London embassy which lasted
as long as Page was in the British capital.

It is possible to set down in a few sentences the major
points of controversy, for they changed little, even though the
dispute lasted several weeks. Grey refused to accept the Declaration because he said it was in several respects obsolete,
not accepted as international law, and harmful to the Allies.
The contraband list it proposed did not take into account the
modern means of warfare. The free list included several items,
such as copper, chemicals, and cotton, now useful in the manufacture of war material which his government never could
place on the contraband list. The Declaration failed to recognize the doctrine of continuous voyage—that the character of
goods rested with their ultimate and not immediate destination.
American products consigned to neutral European states with
land access to Germany—e.g., Holland or Denmark—might
in fact be headed for Germany. Grey insisted that the navy
must intercept such cargo before it reached the neutral state,
or else it could not intercept it at all. The foreign secretary
offered to accept all provisions of the Declaration except those
which applied to contraband and neutral-to-neutral commerce,
and promised to be considerate of American rights.

Lansing could answer some of these objections. He argued
that unless the Allies accepted the Declaration in full, their
enemies would not do so. He pointed out that provisions of
the Declaration allowed expansion of the contraband list, and
in one cable suggested a supplement which would allow the
British some liberty to intercept ships headed for neutral ports.
The one objection to which the counselor had no satisfactory
response was the proposed free list, for the Declaration for-

bade items on this list ever being made contraband. Had Lansing found a strong argument on this latter point it would have made no difference. In constructing a legal basis for American neutrality, the United States had provided a rationale for defeat on this issue. This government could not unilaterally proclaim rules to be international law. To do so would have been illegal, unneutral, contrary to the foundation Wilson wished to establish for American policy. Lansing pressed the Declaration of London no fewer than four times, but in face of British objection, he had to drop the whole scheme. On October 22, 1914, the counselor, with Wilson's approval, sent word to Britain that the United States thereafter would base its rights and claims on previous treaties and international law.

With the failure of the United States to get British adherence to the Declaration, the Anglo-American controversy over neutral rights turned into more obscure arguments. Most of the questions the United States had expected the Declaration of London to answer were now markedly uncertain. Resting its case on existing law, the United States still felt it had grounds for a broad range of activity on the seas. But international law provided only the skimpiest outline; it was vague, left many questions unanswered, and almost none of it was up to date. As American shippers put to sea to engage in what they regarded as legitimate wartime commerce, belligerents —in this case the Allies, and especially Britain—respected only those rights they felt unsafe to ignore. Had it not been for fear of harm the United States could bring to their cause, the British and French would have disregarded American neutral rights altogether.

The war on the seas was nothing more than an extension of the war on land. Fighting had begun on the Continent with offensives on both major fronts to bring about a rapid victory. The German drive in the west came to a halt in early September 1914 when the British and French held the line at the famous Battle of the Marne. By mid-September the Germans had repulsed a Russian advance into East Prussia. The war on both fronts then settled into a gloomy stalemate marked by little mobility and almost unbelievable loss of life. In 1915, for example, the French suffered almost a million and a half casualties and found themselves, at the year's end, in nearly the same battlefield position as they had occupied at the beginning of the year. To carry on this sort of conflict required a willingness to expend manpower resources and the ability to produce or obtain tremendous amounts of supplies and money. For these reasons the United States found itself becoming important in the war. The Allies stepped up orders of all sorts and made arrangements for purchasing some of the supplies on credit. Inasmuch as the Germans were not yet in a position to challenge this traffic, the American participants faced a thoroughly prosperous situation. For producers who filled orders from Germany or Austria-Hungry it was a different story.

Though not as effective as it would become, the British navy by the end of 1914 was able to pass judgment on much of the traffic destined for Europe. Since the major warships were tied up keeping watch on the German fleet, the British commandeered a large number of fast merchantmen or passenger liners, painted them gray, installed several guns—thus making them warships (cruisers)—and sent them into sea lanes to intercept any vessel heading their way. In the American view these vessels were obliged to obey international law pertaining to contraband and search on the sea. They fell considerably short of complying, partly because international law was unrealistic, partly because to do so would have been inconvenient and not fully effective. Britain expanded the list of goods classified as absolute contraband from twelve items in August to twenty-nine in December. Goods ordinarily identified as conditional contraband the British often treated as absolute contraband, and felt no compulsion to prove these items were destined for the German military forces. (Quite the contrary, Britain insisted that American shippers had to prove the goods were not headed for the German army.) The familiar example of this irksome procedure was the treatment of foodstuffs. In October the navy began seizing all food which by any means might reach Germany, despite the fact that some of the goods surely were destined for the civil population. Even more irritating than the seizure of produce consigned to Germany was Britain's interception of goods shipped to neutral European countries. Legally the United States should have been able to trade with these nations in any item it chose. In fact, many of these products never reached the destination. Traditional rules had stipulated that warships must stop and search neutral merchantmen at sea. The British violated this law by taking ships into port where the vessels could undergo a thorough search. In port there might be a long delay, sometimes weeks or even months, and if perishable goods were aboard they spoiled. The shipowner meanwhile lost the use of his vessel. All in all, American war trade was a profitable venture, but individuals engaged in certain types of commerce found themselves subjected to great inconvenience, if not loss of income.

The person held accountable for this troublesome behavior was the British foreign secretary. On Grey's shoulders all American complaints ultimately came to rest, and he was expected to offer satisfactory explanation or promise of relief. It was no easy undertaking, for in his efforts to appease American opinion he could not lose sight of the primary object of stifling German trade. Considering the circumstances, Grey did as well as anyone could. He was careful not to allow measures which would create severe hardship and inspire retaliation in the United States. Aware of a possible collapse of the cotton market and a depression in the southern states, Grey kept cotton off the contraband list and for several months allowed large shipments through to Germany, even though he knew it was useful in manufacture of dynamite. When he found it necessary to seize cargoes, he often instructed the British government to pay for them and tried to hasten on their way ships detained in British harbors. Speaking to the American ambassador in London or sending instructions to Spring-Rice, he sought to defend measures for which he could offer no promise of change. He pointed to the impossibility of searching large modern vessels on the high seas, and to the necessity that inspecting officers be deliberate and thorough. Grey explained that it would be useless to intercept only goods shipped directly to the enemy if Germany could receive the same supplies via transshipment from adjacent neutral states, and pointed to the example of Holland, a nation which normally imported 1,000 tons of copper per year, by October 1914 had received 4,170. The Dutch obviously were sending much of the copper on to the enemy's war machine. Page, who felt these measures reasonable and necessary for the British war effort, argued in cables to Washington that the United States should lodge protests, press for financial settlement of individual cases, and otherwise allow Britain to take action it deemed necessary.

In the United States, beyond the influence of Grey's reasonable and charming manner, people were of a less cooperative mood. While there developed no general unrest at this early stage of the war, British measures of trade restriction did provoke irritation within several important American interest groups. German-Americans and Irish Americans, of course, were much disturbed at anything which might prove beneficial to Britain and France. Those groups finding their economic interests in jeopardy—particularly producers of copper, meat, and some other foodstuffs—sent a huge number of protests to the State Department. The Department passed these cases on to Page, who for various reasons—lack of facts, Grey's evasion, or some technical detail—could obtain only limited satisfaction. Hence, in mid-December, the president and officials in the State Department decided it was necessary to send Britain a general note of protest.

When someone leaked news to the press that the administration was preparing such a move, the note received exaggerated attention, giving rise to anticipation that the United States was going to challenge one of the European belligerents. If the message had gone out as drafted, apparently by Solicitor Cone Johnson, it might have had this effect, but after undergoing the revision of Lansing, Bryan, and finally House and Wilson, it came out the friendliest sort of reminder that Britain should be conscious of American neutral rights. The note surveyed those measures which were illegal or of questionable legality and cautioned that continuation might arouse public opinion. That was about all it said. There appeared no demand that Britain cease any act of trade restriction, no hint of retaliation if the British continued along lines already begun. The note caused not the slightest distress in the Foreign Office. Spring-Rice cabled that Britain should not take the note seriously, because it was mere window-dressing, "for consumption of Congress, German vote and commercial interests," and Grey believed this assessment true.[6] As the foreign secretary prepared a reply to the American message, his principal thought was to reassure the United States government that Britain would remain respectful of American public opinion. He saw no need for weakening the British system, and he promised none.

In other ways during the first months of neutrality the Wilson administration showed itself willing to adjust to the needs of the Allies in their prosecution of the war. In October, as mentioned, the government in an indirect way modified the ban on loans, a decision in which Bryan, Lansing, and Wilson concurred. Presumably the change came for the purpose of allowing credit (in this case to the French government) and not a formal loan; but credit is a type of loan, and the outright tendering of funds was only a step away. While the decision formally rested on legal grounds—the government decided that it had no right to forbid loans—American officials showed a consciousness of the relationship between credit and the growing American prosperity. Without financial assistance the Allies could not continue the huge business with the United States. Needless to say, American credit and loans became a part of the economic link with the Allies and the Allied war effort, although, again, these conditions developed gradually and not because the Wilson administration planned them.

The United States failed to protest when Britain in November declared the North Sea a war zone and began to lay

6. Dec. 29, 1914, Foreign Office Papers, Series 368, Vol. 1162, Public Record Office, London. Hereafter, citations from Foreign Office Papers will read, for example, 368/1162.

mines in large sections of that area. Probably an illegal act, it was said by the British to represent retaliation for Germany's earlier indiscriminate use of mines. The American government remained silent even though the measure greatly strengthened Britain's control of commerce in the North Sea. Ships sailing in the mined areas usually had to stop in the British Isles to obtain sailing instructions through the mine fields. In port, British officials inspected the vessels and halted those cargoes they did not wish to go through.

There was finally the heralded case of the *Dacia,* an episode that for a while seemed to bear the makings of a clash between Britain and the United States. This controversy involved the right of American citizens to purchase German ships which, because of fear of capture by the Royal Navy, had laid up in American harbors. Seemingly the ships were relegated to remaining idle the rest of the war. The American government had authorized the purchase and reregistry of these vessels in August 1914, when the country had faced a pressing need for merchant ships. It was one of the problems for which international law offered no clear solution, and the United States said the transfer was legal. Viewing the transaction as illegal and beneficial to the enemy, the British government repeatedly declared it could not allow passage of these ships if they engaged in trade with Germany. The *Dacia* was important because it was the first interned vessel that put to sea under new ownership and thus was a test of what seemed to be rigid positions of the American and British governments, and because the ship's movement, constantly before the public eye, had inspired a large amount of journalistic expostulation. Presumably a clash over the *Dacia* also would have carried over to other aspects of British-American relations. The controversy ended abruptly in February 1915 when a French cruiser seized the *Dacia* as the vessel neared its destination at Rotterdam. That the French and not the British seized the *Dacia* has been long regarded an example of Grey's careful respect for American opinion—he was afraid to have the British intercept the ship, so the story went—but recent evidence suggests that such was not the case. Grey was prepared to capture the *Da-*

cia, and British ships would have done so had the vessel not happened to travel into the French zone of patrol. The upshot, whatever the method, was that the Allies won their point and again the United States yielded. No other former German ship attempted to carry cargo to Germany.

By the beginning of 1915 the United States had taken its first steps in establishing policies toward the World War. While the president rested the American position on a legal foundation, he found much room for maneuver, and in such circumstances almost every decision the first six months of war had proved beneficial to the Allies. Wilson had showed himself willing to tolerate most British methods of keeping American supplies from the Central Powers. The United States was well on its way to becoming the banker, arsenal, and warehouse for Britain and France. Trade with the Allies, which amounted to $825 million in 1914, by 1916 would soar to four times that amount. Trade with the Central Powers, valued in 1914 at some $170 million, would dwindle by 1916 to about one percent of the former figure.

It might be useful at this stage to review why this situation came about. There was, in the first place, the economic vulnerability of the United States, the desire to continue—if possible, to increase—commerce with the nations at war. The need to trade with Europe was so obvious that virtually no one gave thought to not doing so. The effort—indeed, the United States took these steps so mechanically that there was no single major decision—to promote a lively wartime trade provided the framework for almost all the problems of neutrality; it led to perplexing questions, and the need for Wilson to articulate fine points of international law. It also made inevitable that American neutrality would prove beneficial to the Allies. Even if Wilson had held Britain to a more pro-neutral definition of international law, most American trade would have gone to the Allies, because such had been the prewar pattern of American trade. Moreover, the Allies needed American goods more than did the Central Powers, who were more self-sufficient.

At the same time it is true that Wilson, prompted by advisers, tolerated measures of British trade restriction that neither international law nor the requirements of neutrality would have compelled. It simply was convenient to do so. It was more convenient to allow the British to curtail shipments of goods to Germany and neutral European states than to force them to stop, especially when there was no way of knowing what measures would have been necessary to stop them. Walter Page had said it would take an act of war. On a different course the United States might have found itself entangled in complicated and possibly costly and dangerous problems, the sort of situation Americans expected neutrality to avoid. This tolerant attitude might have been inconvenient and perhaps unacceptable had it been detrimental to the American economy. Such was not the case, because Allied purchases alone were enough to promote prosperity. The other way by which the United States would have been made to suffer from benevolent neutrality was German retaliation, some manner of punishing the United States for its benevolence, and in the first months of war Germany had no such means. Wilson acquiesced in the British system because it seemed the best way of avoiding difficulty, was profitable, and seemed perfectly safe; and the president could reconcile his stand with his own interpretation of legal neutrality. The results, moreover, were consistent with his personal feeling about the war.

The most intriguing—and difficult to assess—aspect of neutrality policies is the effect of Wilson's personal thoughts. He undeniably was sympathetic to the Allies. He admired British culture and institutions, knew and trusted several of the British leaders, and while he rarely spoke about issues of the war, now and then revealed to friends that he fell short of "neutrality in thought." House's diary of August 1914 carried the statement, "He goes even further than I in his condemnation of Germany's part in this war, and almost allows his feeling to include the German people as a whole rather than the leaders alone." [7] And to Spring-Rice, Wilson once confided:

7. Aug. 30, 1914, Seymour, *The Intimate Papers of Colonel House,* I, 293.

"Everything that I love most in the world is at stake. . . . If they [the Germans] succeed, we shall be forced to take such measures of defence here as would be fatal to our form of Government and American ideals." [8] Wilson at the same time struggled to prevent his feelings from influencing policy; his private and public utterances include many other statements which professed detachment and neutrality. One easily can find reasons other than Wilson's bias to explain why American policy functioned in a manner favoring the Allies. Does this mean that Wilson's feeling played no part in establishing the foundations of American neutrality? It never will be possible to say with certainty. If one could have removed those accidental factors which promoted commercial relations between the United States and Britain and France, and let the president's emotions stand alone, or if one could have had Germany and Britain change places, allowing the United States the chance to act in a manner beneficial to the Germans, it might be possible to test the effect of Wilson's bias. The most one can say about such hypothetical circumstances is that the president would have faced decisions much more agonizing than those in 1914 and the first days of 1915.

Agonizing decisions were to come anyway, for however much Wilson favored the Allies, however beneficial his policies to those nations, he certainly did not wish to join them in war. He was convinced in 1915 no less than in 1914 that neutrality—as he interpreted it—was best for the United States. He had allowed Britain large liberty with American trade but could not, and did not wish to, allow the British to do fully as they pleased. The president had to consider American opinion, which became much disturbed over British behavior in 1915, and he had to have something to hold up to the Germans as evidence of American neutrality. The Germans, who in 1915 found a means of retaliation, were ever anxious to see this evidence.

8. Ambassador Spring-Rice to Sir Edward Grey, Sept. 3, 1914, Grey Papers.

3

Neutrality Assailed from Both Sides

IT IS wholly possible to muster understanding and perhaps a touch of sympathy for the frustration Germans felt with the war on the high seas. After years of excited attention and a huge expenditure of funds, they had built a large, modern, efficient navy and could take pride that Germany at last was a major naval power. But when the war came, of what use were all these vessels? Still smaller than Britain's navy, the High Seas Fleet kept to port almost all the war. Britannia ruled the waves as never before, almost as if there were no German navy. Particularly frustrating was the use Britain was making of sea power as a means of controlling commerce. While German editorial writers and government officials might direct verbal attacks on the contraband trade from America, they knew that this traffic was fully legitimate, the sort of enterprise in which Germans at other times had participated. The problem was that Germany lacked the means to stop this traffic. Britain's interception of legitimate German trade was a somewhat different matter, and Germans felt they should be able to expect some diplomatic assistance from neutral nations, especially the United States. By the beginning of 1915 there was no evidence the help would be forthcoming. Enraged at what the British did on the seas, angry at Americans for allowing them to do it, the Germans seemingly could only watch and accept a situation they could not change.

The German admiralty was slow to discover that submarines might be the way to compensate for an inferior surface fleet. Not exactly a new weapon at the start of the war, these vessels—U-boats, or "undersea boats" (*Unterseebooten*), they were called—had yet to prove themselves as an effective means of warfare. About two hundred feet long, displacing perhaps six hundred tons, they were not an imposing sight. Much of the boat rode beneath the water even when surfaced, and except for the conning tower, it scarcely was visible from a distance. Few men who served in a submarine's crew were anxious to advance its reputation, for working conditions were incredibly bad. Food and supplies were stashed anywhere one could find a hole, even on top of the torpedoes; there was barely room for the thirty-five or so sailors who manned the vessel. The air was clammy with the smell of machine oil and carbonic gas, not to mention cooking and human odors, and an officer who decided to light up a cigar was in a sense imposing his habit on all the people aboard. Small wonder that German admirals who spoke of the fleet swelled with dignity at mention of the mighty surface ships, the dreadnoughts; these were the ships navies were made of. And the little submarines with their thin hulls and single gun on the deck seemed the tiniest, albeit the most mysterious, part of the armadas of that day.

Germany had submarines because other navies had them, and in 1914 Britain and even the United States possessed more of these vessels then did the kaiser's navy. Naval officials regarded them simply as unusual warships, their function being to do battle with the enemy's men-of-war. At the start of war, submarines performed little of this limited activity, for Germany had few available for duty, and with the fleet in harbor there was no emphasis on the war at sea.

Then gradually a new hope arose. On September 5, 1914, a U-boat sank a British warship. Three weeks later German newspapers blazoned with headlines that in a single day a submarine, the *U 9*, had destroyed three British battle cruisers. The *U 9* had caught the *Aboukir,* a vessel of twelve thousand tons, without escort, and sunk it with torpedoes. The submarine simply lay in wait as a second crusier, the *Hogue,* arrived on the scene to assist survivors thrashing about in the cold Atlantic waters, and then the *Cressy,* assuming the submarine had gone, came to investigate the second sinking. It had been, of course, an exceptional combination of good luck and remarkably careless British seamanship, but this fact did not diminish the excitement the *U 9* aroused in Berlin. "We are all delighted . . . , the Kaiser is in seventh heaven," a German admiral noted on hearing the news.[1]

It was inevitable that the German government would advance to the idea of using submarines against enemy commerce, for in this capacity U-boats could have the most costly effect upon battles on the Continent. The Allies, especially Britain, were heavily dependent upon supplies from abroad, and an effective sea campaign could damage them far more than it could Germany. If they could sink warships, submarines should find slow-moving and often defenseless merchantmen easy targets. This unusual warfare might raise moral and legal questions, but those Germans who suffered moral discomfort could set their minds at ease by pointing to Britain's reprehensible methods of warfare. "America has not raised her voice in protest and has taken little or no action against England's closing of the North Sea to neutral shipping," blurted out Admiral Alfred von Tirpitz, secretary of state for naval affairs. "What will America say if Germany declares submarine war on all the enemy's merchant ships? Why not? England wants to starve us. We can play the same game. We can bottle her up and torpedo every English or Allies' ship which nears any harbor in Great Britain." [2]

The major obstacle to such a move, as Tirpitz hinted, was

1. Walter Goerlitz, ed., *The Kaiser and His Court: The Diaries, Note Books and Letters of Admiral Georg Alexander Von Müller, Chief of the Naval Cabinet, 1914–1918* (London, 1961), 34.
2. Published in New York *World,* Dec. 24, 1914, cited in Arthur S. Link, *Wilson: The Struggle for Neutrality, 1914–1915* (Princeton, N. J., 1960), 314–15.

the attitude of neutrals, especially the United States, for it was possible that a broad submarine campaign would cost American lives and property, provoke anger and ultimately American intervention. So argued Theobald von Bethmann Hollweg, chancellor and formal head of the kaiser's government. The submarine issue in 1915 touched off a quarrel within the German government that would continue throughout the period of American neutrality. In the broadest sense the conflict pitted civil officials against high military officers and raised questions familiar to most governments: in time of war, to what extent should military matters influence questions also political and diplomatic? In final analysis should military officials be allowed to guide the nation? Decisions on submarine policy might have been a simple matter had there been clear allocation of authority in the German state. As matters stood the government was remarkably complex, and the power of decision shifted with personality and circumstances.

Much of the confusion stemmed from the condition of the monarchy in Wilhelmian Germany. The face of Kaiser Wilhelm II, with the high cheekbones and mustache tapered upward on the ends, was familiar in all Western countries. By having himself portrayed on a dashing charger or in full military dress with spiked helmet, Wilhelm wanted to appear fierce, strong, and resolute, and to maintain the image long afforded the Prussian monarch. (His facial features were such, however, that with slight distortion, raising the eyebrows, cartoonists easily could give him an appearance of fright.) While the kaiser was not an absolute divine-right monarch, he liked to invoke his association with God and did have great authority in guiding the German war effort. Besides having influence over his ministers and within parliament, he was Supreme Warlord, commander-in-chief of the army and navy. Wilhelm had wanted to be a wise and strong ruler; but being emperor never had been easy, and it was far too large an undertaking for a man with his intellectual and emotional shortcomings. Identified in Allied nations as an impetuous saber-rattler, he was in fact weak, moody, insecure. Unable to devise policy, he left the task of governing to subordinates, contenting himself with approving major decisions. He yielded easily to forceful argument, and if both sides were forceful he found himself in a state of agonizing indecision.

With the kaiser incapable of governing, the responsibility for foreign policy formally rested with the chancellor, Bethmann Hollweg. Vacillating on many matters of state, Bethmann on the submarine issue was clear and consistent. While he never questioned Germany's right, under the rule of reprisal, to use submarines any way it wished, he felt that his nation would face catastrophe if a U-boat campaign provoked American intervention on the side of the Allies. Had he had his way Germany would have exercised utmost caution in using submarines, and the United States might not have been brought into the war. The chancellor unfortunately did not have full authority to guide the German state, or even the executive branch. His power depended upon retaining approval of the kaiser, no easy undertaking with a man who changed his mind so much. He had to be responsive to trends in public opinion and in the legislature, particularly the aristocratic upper house, for he was aware that sharp public criticism could bring down his regime. Finally, political and diplomatic matters often affected prosecution of the war, in which cases Bethmann had to compete for authority with high military officers.

There is no need to elaborate on the position military officials had held in German society and government. A favorite quip of an earlier time had been that whereas most states had armies, the Prussian army had a state. If that situation had ceased to exist by 1914, the military establishment still was influential. High-ranking officers carried much of the nation's prestige and social glamor; the kaiser liked to surround himself with military men and tried to appear one himself. The generals could point to past contribution to German strength and unity and could claim—as can any nation's military establishment in time of war—that preservation of the state depended upon placing military consideration first. Had the military been of one mind during the period of American neutrality, Bethmann would have had little chance to control foreign policy.

Fortunately, there were differences among the officers which strengthened Bethmann's hand in guiding policy with the United States. The chancellor's toughest adversary, the loudest advocate of submarine warfare, was Grand Admiral Alfred von Tirpitz, Germany's most prestigious sailor. Distinguishable by flashy braid and a scraggly white beard, Tirpitz was a bold, gruff old man, "a dreamer," remarked a colleague, "who refuses to accept any opinion that conflicts with his own." [3] Convinced of his infallibility, the Grand Admiral was willing to use virtually any device to bend the kaiser to his will. In the first year of the war Tirpitz was ably assisted by Admiral Gustav Bachmann, head of the admiralty. While almost all admirals agreed with their superior officers on submarine warfare, they did not have access to the throne and had to work through Bachmann and Tirpitz. The Chief of the General Staff in 1915 was General Erich von Falkenhayn. Theoretically an equal of Tirpitz, Falkenhayn in fact was more influential, because of traditional German reliance upon the army and because the First World War was essentially a land conflict. To Bethmann's good fortune, Falkenhayn had his mind on his armies. He showed some hesitation to mingle in political affairs and much of the time endorsed the chancellor's argument that the United States must be kept out of the conflict. Though foreign policy technically remained the responsibility of the chancellor and his foreign minister, each major decision on relations with the United States had to be fought out with the military chieftains. Generally the submarine issue pitted the civil government against the navy, with the army a powerful interested bystander. Decisions depended upon the condition of the war, the ability to manipulate and muster strong argument and, finally, to capture the mind of a whimsical monarch. Understandably, the course of submarine warfare frequently changed.

3. Goerlitz, *The Kaiser and His Court,* 29.

Persons favoring a campaign against commercial shipping in 1915 brushed away the threat of United States intervention with not altogether convincing arguments. Neutral nations would not become involved, they said, because fear of submarines would drive their ships out of the zone of operation. Even if the United States did experience losses, that nation was not prepared to declare war, nor could it be, for American opinion was so divided that the government could not bring itself to a far-reaching policy. The Germans generally felt an urge to use a new, perhaps decisive, weapon. Pressure was so strong from military and public officials that Bethmann probably could not have resisted it long. Besides, he was not convinced at this early stage that the move was unwise. One never could know what the United States would do until it faced the problems of submarine warfare. The chancellor thus approved, as did Kaiser Wilhelm, announcement on February 4, 1915, of a submarine campaign in waters around the British isles. While the Germans planned to strike at enemy ships, the message warned that there could result accidental loss of neutral vessels or lives.

The German message raised for the United States important and perplexing questions. Submarine warfare represented a sharp departure from past practices of sea warfare and a violation of international law. The Germans, of course, had as much right as the British to stop commerce, including American vessels, from going to the enemy, but the rules of warfare required belligerent ships to stop their prey at sea. If contraband was aboard, belligerents had the right to confiscate or destroy it. They had no right to destroy the ship, if it was neutral, and were required to assure the safety of all persons aboard. The submarine practice of attacking without warning automatically violated these rules and probably, because of the difficulty in establishing a ship's identity, endangered American lives and property. It was possible to argue that international law was unrealistic because it did not take into account the way submarines operated. If the United States had accepted that proposition, the government could have followed one of two courses: allow Americans and American property to enter European waters without the government's blessing, or with only formal support; order all Americans and American ships out of the danger zone. Either alternative would have entailed an abandonment of neutral rights and international law; either would have been economically costly, unpopular with American public opinion, and, in Wilson's estimate, morally degrading.

Wilson thus undertook the difficult chore of resting policy on international law, however vague and poorly applicable to modern warfare. He probably would have allowed the Germans some minor changes, as he was doing with the British; but submarine warfare was not a minor innovation. It was drastic, deadly, and if accepted would have rendered useless all efforts to promote neutral rights and defend the lives of non-combatants. Wilson supported international law because it was a device for protecting American interests and honor, and for discharging his constitutional duties. It also was an ideal he would have liked to see accepted by all nations. As leader of the most powerful neutral nation he felt an obligation to try to preserve for the world some semblance of order and sanity. There seemed no one else to do it. Even so, Wilson had limited goals in his reply to Germany of February 10. If he regarded submarine warfare as illegal and inhumane, and hoped his influence would discourage its use, he did not feel the authority to tell belligerents which weapons they could or could not use, and hoped to avoid policy so decisive that it would range the United States on one side. The note did not challenge submarine policy as a whole, although it reminded the Germans of the rule of visit and search—the requirement to stop and search ships at sea before condemning them—and said that sudden attacks would be "so unprecedented in naval warfare that this Government is reluctant to believe that the Imperial Government contemplates [them] as possible." With respect to American ships and the lives of American citizens, Wilson left the impression that submarine warfare was intolerable. He promised to take "any steps necessary to safeguard American lives and property," and to hold Germany to a "strict accountability" for violation of neutral rights.[4]

As far as the message went, it was strong. The United States would not allow attacks on American ships, presumably even if it meant war, although in 1915 that possibility seemed remote. Protection of American lives was more complicated. Did this mean only persons on American ships, or include American nationals on belligerent (probably British) passenger vessels or merchantmen? Americans as a matter of course took passage on foreign liners. Merchantmen often carried a few passengers, and it was not unusual for Yankees to find employment on British freighters. Did the United States intend to protect these citizens? If the ships were armed, did this make a difference? Wilson did not have answers to these questions, if indeed he thought of them. Nor did the Germans know exactly what Wilson had meant. However firm the message had seemed, the president's pacific tendencies were well known in Germany, and observation of relations with Britain had convinced many German officials that Wilson would endure almost any injury rather than lead the United States into war. They were willing at least to test the president's will.

So, as it turned out, were the Allies, who viewed the German proclamation of submarine warfare as a stroke of good fortune. Feeling that submarines at that time posed no great threat to their shipping, Britain and France were pleased to find an issue which might cause difficulty between the United States and the enemy. The Allies also saw the German proclamation as a lever for greater restriction on neutral commerce with the Central Powers. They now could defend, on grounds of retaliation, measures previously felt unsafe to impose on the United States—or so Grey thought. At the same time they hoped to show clear contrast between peaceful Allied methods of economic warfare and barbarous sudden attacks by submarines. The German proclamation sent the British and

4. The secretary of state to Ambassador Gerard, Feb. 10, 1915, *Papers Relating to the Foreign Relations of the United States, 1915, Supplement* (Washington, D.C., 1928), 98–100.

French into consultation, from which emerged a new plan for strangulation of trade with the enemy. Made public by a British proclamation on March 1, 1915, and put into effect by an Order in Council on March 11, the program pledged to "prevent commodities of any kind from reaching or leaving Germany," and if necessary "to detain and take into ports ships carrying goods of presumed enemy destination, ownership or origin." [5]

While the proclamation much resembled a blockade, the Allies avoided use of that word, because in a strict sense they could not meet the specifications set out in international law.[6] Under traditional conditions of blockade, warships stationed themselves outside and sealed off enemy ports from all traffic. The problem in 1915 was that most trade with Germany went through neutral ports, the closing of which would be legally indefensible and so costly to neutral states as to invite retaliation. Instead of closing ports, the Allies placed warships at sea, cruising perhaps fifteen or twenty miles apart, near enough so that they could intercept any vessel attempting to pass by. If inspecting officers found evidence that the produce was for use in the neutral country, they let it through. If there arose the slightest suspicion that the cargo might be useful to Germany, a cruiser accompanied it to a British port, where government officials probably would confiscate or purchase the goods. The procedure was of dubious legality and almost certainly injurious to some American economic groups. Had the Wilson administration chosen, it could have found grounds for spirited opposition.

The administration chose not to stand up to the Order in

5. The British ambassador to the secretary of state, March 1, 1915, *ibid.,* 127–28.
6. International law specified that for a blockade to be legal, it had to be effective. That is, the blockading nation had to have enough ships present in the area to keep all vessels out. Otherwise, neutral nations were not obliged to honor the decree. The Allies avoided proclaiming a blockade because they did not have enough ships to make it fully effective, and because, as mentioned, they did not wish to place themselves in the position of formally blockading neutral nations.

Council, at least not yet. "We are face to face with something they are going to do," Wilson wrote Bryan, "and they are going to do it no matter what representations we make." [7] The president then wrote a formal reply to the Allied proclamation, in which he merely pointed out inconsistencies in the Allied position and reminded Britain and France of American neutral rights. The purpose of the message was partly to lay the basis for financial claims, partly to express Wilson's optimistic interpretation of the Allied proclamation. He was hopeful that Britain and France would go to great length to allow American trade with continental Europe.

Hence by the spring of 1915 American neutrality faced a simultaneous challenge from both groups of belligerents in their efforts to keep supplies from the enemy. Some scholars have suggested that Wilson thereupon attempted to adjust American policy to both the British and German methods of economic warfare. Even though the president would have preferred that course, one must doubt if such was the intent—it certainly was not the result. The note to Germany on submarine warfare was stronger than the message on the blockade. Though it contained no threat, it did suggest there were acts the United States government could not tolerate. Diplomatic dispatches have no full meaning until put to the test of events. The note to Britain of March 1915 in a sense had been tested; Wilson sought accommodation along lines laid down the weeks before. It remained to be seen if he would adjust as freely to the tactics Germany planned on the sea.

Some three months would pass before Wilson had to make painful decisions on submarine warfare. U-boats in the meantime made slow progress in their assault on enemy shipping. Germany had only two submarines in the war zone at the time of the proclamation in February, and while construction of new vessels had begun, it took at least twelve months to make them ready for duty. The few incidents which did take place

7. March 24, 1915, *Papers Relating to the Foreign Relations of the United States, The Lansing Papers, 1914–1920* (2 vols., Washington, 1939–40), I, 288–89.

during these weeks—some three or four touched upon matters of American lives and property—posed such new, perplexing problems that the administration could not decide what to do. Lansing, who generally viewed submarine warfare as illegal and barbarous, wished to take firm action in all matters of American right and interest. Already seized by fear of war, Bryan wanted conciliation, and above all to avoid a sharp diplomatic exchange which might swell to a break in relations with Germany. Wilson wanted the best of both positions—the respect for American rights that Lansing pressed, the peace Bryan so desperately sought. How to obtain both was the problem. The first submarine incidents presented such complicated, technical questions that by May of 1915 Wilson had not elaborated publicly on his general statement of February 10.

German officials also faced perplexing decisions. While most naval officers experienced little discomfort from Wilson's submarine message, Chancellor Bethmann carefully mulled over the note, uncertain of hcw far he should let the submarine campaign go. As summer approached, submarine commanders sailed under orders to attack enemy ships and, when possible, spare vessels of neutral nations. The greatest dangers were that neutral citizens might be aboard ships of enemy nations and that there was a high possibility of mistaken attack on a neutral ship.

As fate would have it, the submarine controversy did not procede along a gradual, undramatic course—as had been the case in American dealings with Britain—but German-American relations were suddenly struck by an event so tragic and sensational as to obscure all happenings on the battlefields at that time. On May 7, 1915, a German submarine sank the Cunard liner *Lusitania* as it neared the end of its run from New York to Liverpool. The commander who sent the torpedo into her side, Walther Schweiger, knew he was firing at a large passenger liner, although he did not know if it was the *Lusitania* or her sister, the *Mauretania,* a slightly larger vessel recently pressed into government service as an auxiliary cruiser. He acted fully within authority granted by the government as part of a movement to satisfy military interests and press submarine warfare as far as possible. The great British ship suffered an unusually large explosion and sank within a few minutes, taking with it almost twelve hundred lives, of whom one hundred twenty-four were American.

Technical aspects of the sinking were subject to debate. The attack was illegal if one based legality on traditional maritime practice, under which all vessels but warships were to be confronted on the basis of visit and search. Nations before this time had used only surface vessels, and so the rules of warfare pertained to the way cruisers operated. Germany had argued that submarines could not operate under these rules, for the efficiency of these ships depended largely on their freedom to attack without warning. Surfaced submarines were highly vulnerable, either to gunfire or to ramming by the huge prows of merchant or passenger ships. Britain had asserted the right to change sea rules to meet the needs of modern warfare, and now Germany was demanding—to be sure, in a much larger way—the same right. The *Lusitania* carried contraband —it had forty-two hundred cases of cartridges in the hold— and to the Germans this fact made the attack justifiable.[8] By the old rules it nonetheless was illegal. The sinking tested the ability of Americans to take passage on belligerent ships. International law had not treated this issue, and before the start of submarine warfare it had been no major problem. Americans had no legal right to travel on ships of nations at war; at the same time they were not necessarily under obligation to keep off. Germany had no right to attack people who did not do so. Had the United States come upon this issue in a quieter way, the government probably would have approached it in like manner and possibly taken a position less rigid than it did.

Associated with the dramatic sinking of the *Lusitania,* these matters became enmeshed with questions of morality,

8. The submarine commander did not know of contraband aboard the *Lusitania*. But inasmuch as he was authorized to attack all Allied ships without determining the cargo, it made no difference.

national honor, and prestige. Over thirty thousand tons in displacement, nearly eight hundred feet long, the *Lusitania* was a giant for its day. The ship was a luxury liner, the symbol of prestigious and peaceful travel on the Atlantic. For days after the sinking, Americans were reading accounts of horror and heroism, and of the almost unbelievable speed with which the ship went down. Even though the torpedo had torn a huge hole in the starboard side and caused an enormous expulsion of smoke and steam, many people aboard, including much of the ship's company, were unaware of the acute danger—the *Lusitania,* like the unfortunate *Titanic* before it, had been broadcast as an unsinkable ship—and precious minutes were lost in the beginning. With the rush of water into the hull far below the decorative top decks, and the ship's sharp list to starboard, panic-stricken passengers rushed to find lifejackets or places where the lifeboats were supposed to be. "They must have lost their heads," noted Commander Schweiger upon viewing the scene in his periscope. "Many boats crowded come down bow first or stern first in the water and immediately fill and sink. Fewer lifeboats can be made clear owing to the slant of the boat. . . ." [9] Within fifteen minutes after being struck the ship started its plunge. The *Lusitania* was so long that the bow struck bottom, thrust into the mud, and for a few moments the ship stood poised almost on end, half under, half above water, the fantail raised a hundred feet in the air, the four giant propellors, now motionless, fully visible to the few terrified passengers who chanced to look up from their efforts to stay afloat in the water. The liner then crashed beneath the surface, leaving wreckage of all sorts, the fortunate people able to survive the disaster, and a large number of floating bodies.

No person who read of these events could fail to experience thoughts of distress and astonishment; few could avoid feeling hostility for the nation responsible. It seemed unthinkable that a civilized state could be capable of so savage an

9. A. A. and Mary Hoehling, *The Last Voyage of the Lusitania* (New York, 1956), 113.

attack on defenseless human beings. If the Germans would sink the *Lusitania,* would they respect any human right? "Piracy," thundered Theodore Roosevelt, "piracy on a vaster scale of murder than old-time pirates ever practiced." [10] Of course, not everyone reacted with cries of outrage. Some people in the United States did not know what the *Lusitania* was or what its sinking meant. German-Americans and some coldly detached persons sought to excuse the act as provoked by the British contraband traffic. But these dissenting views did not change the fact that the sinking was one of the most important events of the period of neutrality. It resurrected charges of German brutality which had circulated at the time of the invasion of Belgium, and more than ever they now became believable. It inspired a nationalist movement for retaliation. For the first time many Americans began to consider the possibility that their nation might have to take part in a war that previously had seemed distant. Although submarine attacks became, in time, a standard tactic of "modern" warfare, as did the random bombing of cities, both were regarded as inhumane when initially used during the First World War. Wilson functioned within the atmosphere of 1915, not a half-century later, and at that time the reaction to the sinking of the *Lusitania* was so intense that he had no choice but to do something.

From his advisers the president received conflicting counsel. Secretary of State Bryan was deeply troubled. If he deplored the attack on the *Lusitania,* he worried even more that jingoist agitation would stampede the nation to a hasty declaration of hostilities. Bryan's ideas on submarine warfare are of some interest, for they represented an alternative to Wilson's policy, a course which after the war impressed many as preferable to that which the United States took. The secretary felt a protest to Germany necessary, but he wished it to be conciliatory, and to assure the Germans that the United States did not regard war as a possibility. He also favored sending a note

10. Cited in William H. Harbaugh, *Power and Responsibility: The Life and Times of Theodore Roosevelt* (New York, 1961), 476.

to Britain as evidence of American impartiality. Bryan's most important proposals were his suggestions that Americans be kept off belligerent ships and out of the war zone. These measures seemed to deal with the most pressing problems in the German-American controversy, and if adopted probably would have prevented recurrence of a crisis similar to the *Lusitania* incident. They would have placed on the United States responsibility for avoiding dangerous incidents and moved the government a good distance toward acceptance of submarine warfare.

What Bryan advised was possible if the United States had been willing to accept the consequences. Had the secretary's ideas prevailed, all trade with Britain and France in American ships would have come to a halt, and this important traffic been voluntarily swept from the sea. If the United States failed to challenge this feature of submarine warfare, there would have been no reason to challenge any aspect (if the United States did not take issue with the sinking of American ships, why should it take issue with the sinking of British ships or vessels of other neutral nations?); freed of any government restraint, submarines would have taken a heavier toll of American goods shipped in belligerent merchantmen. If the United States refused to challenge interference by submarine, it would have been absurd to challenge interference by cruiser, and Britain would have exercised a free hand in curtailing American commerce with continental Europe. American trade would have become a pawn in the war at sea, each side attempting to capture or destroy more than the other. Even if one disregarded considerations of prestige and honor—themselves no small matters—and the effect on the war, the economic consequences would have been great. Bryan correctly assessed the danger submarines posed for American neutrality, but he could offer no better alternative than submission. He was so obsessed with peace that he was willing to give away what could be the most effective device for maintaining peace: the threat of forceful retaliatory response. Individuals might find it possible to turn the other cheek; nations, particularly proud and powerful ones, rarely have done so.

If Bryan's ideas represented one extreme course for the United States, the other extreme called for the issuance of a simple, direct ultimatum: Germany must yield or face war. A few Americans decided that no measure short of war, or a message that likely would lead to war, could satisfactorily uphold national honor or punish Germany for its wrongful ways. Page's cables from London spoke favorably of a declaration of hostilities, and Colonel House, also in the British capital (and, incidentally, also in the company of Edward Grey), expressed some of the same thoughts. "I believe an immediate demand should be made upon Germany for assurance that this shall not occur again," he cabled Wilson. "If she fails to give such assurance, I should inform her that our Government expected to take such measures as were necessary to ensure the safety of American citizens. If war follows, it will not be a new war, but an endeavor to end more speedily an old one. Our intervention will save, rather than increase, the loss of life." [11] This approach, which appealed to Anglophiles and strong nationalists, was tempting in view of the great emotional outpouring over the destruction of the *Lusitania*. It also was the most risky response. If Germany refused, the United States would have to follow through on its threat or suffer the humiliation of backing down. Blunt messages are always dangerous, especially when sent to a proud and powerful nation such as Germany, which might have felt constrained to reply in like manner. The note, not the original dispute, would have become the issue. It would have been a hasty response, and the only persons who favored that approach were those anxious to go to war. Most of the American population favored a course less far-reaching and immeasurably more difficult to arrange. They wanted the fullest measure of satisfaction from the Germans, but also expected the government to keep them out of war.

Wilson needed no prompting along these lines, for his objects were the same as those of most of his countrymen.

11. May 9, 1915, Seymour, *The Intimate Papers of Colonel House,* I, 434.

Shocked with the sinking, thinking it brutal, an intolerable attack on American citizens and a crime against humanity, he was no less convinced that a declaration of war, or an act that quickly would lead to war, was hasty, needless, contrary to the interests of the United States. Besides sending his nation's sons into the bloody slaughter, he would be relegating the United States to a position of simply another belligerent, no better than the rest. The world thereby would lose the sane, progressive leadership that could be provided only by a powerful, disinterested nation—a role Wilson had come to envision for the United States and himself. If war was not the answer, neither was surrender. Wilson rejected all Bryan's suggestions because he feared they would weaken American demands and sacrifice national prestige. To buckle before German military pressure, he felt, would leave him derelict in his duties as president, open the door for more violation of American rights, and compromise his position as leader of world moral opinion. Wilson realized that he could expect little help from House and others seemingly anxious to take the United States into the war. Lansing contributed needed information on law and precedent, but Wilson took the task of composing a response to the Germans largely upon himself. He spent much time alone; to give an appearance of calm he played golf one afternoon, and as if to anticipate criticism for not acting sooner or more strongly, he spoke at Philadelphia on May 10 of a nation being "too proud to fight." He doubtless took comfort in feeling that public opinion was on his side, but even had the people been of a different mood, he probably would have done as he did.

The *Lusitania* note went out on May 13, approximately a week after the sinking took place. Bryan signed it with a "heavy heart" because he believed it dangerously rigid. The note followed the pattern Wilson earlier had used to deal with submarine warfare. If he pitched his argument on a high moral plane, and lectured the Germans on their responsibilities to civilization, he made a distinction between changes he would like to see and demands he felt compelled to make on behalf

of the United States. The note condemned the sinking of the
Lusitania; asked for apology, reparation, promise that the
deed would not recur; and for the first time asserted an American right to travel on belligerent liners and merchantmen.
Speaking for the "sacred principles of justice and humanity,"
Wilson expressed doubt that submarines could safely be used
as destroyers of commerce and suggested, although he did
not feel he had the right to demand this change, that Germany
should give up submarine warfare altogether. While the message reiterated the government's intent to protect all American
neutral rights, it contained no ultimatum, no threat, and im-
plied that the submarine question was a matter for diplomacy
and not war.

The German government was unwilling to do as Wilson
asked. The admiralty was as adamant as ever in its demands
on submarine warfare, and the sinking of the *Lusitania* was by
no means unpopular with German public opinion. The regret
some Germans felt at the death of so many innocent passengers
was a small matter beside the excitement of knowing that a
tiny U-boat had struck down the giant of the Atlantic. Finding
a clear relation between the sinking and the munitions traffic,
German opinion was not favorable to concession. Bethmann
understood this fact no less than he understood the danger of
provoking the hostility of the United States. On May 9 he had
sent neutral governments a promise that submarines would
take special precaution to avoid striking neutral ships, and that
seemed about as far as he could go. The chancellor, besides,
had received news about a conference in Washington between
the Austro-Hungarian ambassador and the secretary of state,
in which Bryan had intimated that the American note was
partly a response to public opinion, that the American government did not contemplate any stronger action. Conditions at
home and abroad all pointed to the wisdom of an evasive answer to the United States, a message designed to drag out debate while emotions cooled. The German note of May 29
offered little except regret at the great loss of life. It spoke of
Britain's atrocious campaign to starve the German population,

argued that the presence of contraband aboard the *Lusitania* justified its sinking, stressed the need for both governments to obtain more facts. The message did not offer to abandon submarine warfare.

From all appearances the *Lusitania* controversy then settled into an intellectual debate over details and moral aspects of submarine warfare. Wilson sent three notes to Germany during the summer of 1915, and the German government replied with two. In his presentation Wilson persisted in the argument that submarines abide by rules of cruiser warfare, although, with some inconsistency, he sidestepped the issue of Americans traveling on belligerent merchantmen, and in writing the third note came to focus on the question of travel on passenger liners. Though Germany had yielded to none of his demands, Wilson was not fully displeased with the course of negotiation. He felt he had stood on principle and believed it possible that Germany secretly might have made those changes it publicly would not admit. The strongest message was the third note, dispatched July 8, which warned that the American government would regard another attack on a passenger ship as "deliberately unfriendly." [12]

The administration's policy did not please all sections of American opinion. Bryan resigned rather than sign the second *Lusitania* note, and was replaced shortly thereafter by Robert Lansing. He objected not so much to the note as to unwillingness to supplement it in ways he had suggested, fearing that German-American relations would become a see-saw diplomatic exchange, each note stronger than the one before it, while neither side took measures to remove the causes of tension. The secretary, moreover, had long experienced a hurt feeling over his standing in the government and with the president. Since the war had started Wilson had consistently rejected Bryan's advice and turned to other members of the administration. "Colonel House has been Secretary of State, not I," he said to the president, his lip quivering with emo-

12. The secretary of state to Ambassador Gerard, July 21, 1915, *For. Rels., 1915, Supp.,* 419–21.

tion. "I have never had your full confidence." [13] Outside the government Bryan became the spokesman for some of those factions willing to try virtually any measure to preserve peace with Germany.

Criticism was even sharper from persons who represented the other extreme of American policy. They were mostly pro-Ally, highly nationalistic, and sensitive to anything resembling an infringement of American rights and honor, at least when it came from the Germans. Willing to accept war after the sinking of the *Lusitania,* perhaps even anxious to have intervention come about, they believed Wilson guilty of no less than letting the Germans get away with murder. These individuals found moments of satisfaction during the long submarine controversy, but much of the time they grumbled that American policy was too soft, and increasingly found the problem in the president. If Wilson was not a coward, they thought, at least he lacked those stalwart fighting qualities that had made the United States a large and powerful nation. They pictured him as the lofty professor who expounded principle and composed eloquent diplomatic notes when he should have been about the more forceful and earthy business of putting the Germans in their place.

The best-known representative of this point of view was Theodore Roosevelt. The Rough Rider had all the qualities of thought and temperament which encouraged opposition to Wilson's German policy. An Anglophile, strongly nationalistic and having at times what seemed an almost adolescent fascination for military solution, Roosevelt also was a Republican and never forgot that the president would be running for re-election in 1916. He developed an intense dislike for Wilson and could not stomach the thought of that man speaking for the United States. "Did you notice what its . . . number was?" Roosevelt cynically asked a relative on hearing that Wilson had sent another note to Germany. "I fear I have lost track

13. So Wilson told House, House Diary, June 24, 1915; see also Ernest R. May, *The World War and American Isolation 1914–1917* (Cambridge, Mass., 1959), 155.

myself; but I am inclined to think it is No. 11,765, Series B." [14] In a more verbose mood Roosevelt wrote that Wilson belonged to a group of "professional pacifists, . . . flubdubs and mollycoddles . . . every soft creature, every coward and weakling, every man who can't look more than six inches ahead, every man whose god is money, or pleasure, or ease." [15]

Thus American opinion, divided at the start of the war, underwent a sharper division and certainly greater fluidity as the result of submarine warfare. If the people generally were more anti-German after the sinking of the *Lusitania,* they were far from certain where such thoughts should lead them. At times of crisis or triumph, Wilson could count on huge surges of popular support. Once the crisis passed or the triumph seemed tarnished by some new event, critics renewed the attack on aspects of policy. In a way these conditions made determination of policy a complex and delicate matter. Critics did raise questions and hold alternatives before the public. Wilson was sensitive to criticism. In another sense the presence of extremist opposition groups made Wilson's road more appealing. They inclined people toward the middle. While one group promised peace for the United States and the other a strict respect for American rights, neither could offer its goal without placing the other in jeopardy. Wilson pledged himself to provide both.

In late summer of 1915, with the *Lusitania* controversy in a state of indefinite suspension, the submarine issue took a sharp new turn when on August 19 a U-boat sank the British liner *Arabic.* Bound westward from Liverpool, the ship could not have been carrying contraband. Although only two Americans lost their lives, the attack presented for Wilson a situation even more critical than the sinking of the *Lusitania.* A refusal to grant major concession to the United States would mean that Germany had decided to ignore warnings laid down in the

14. Cited in Henry F. Pringle, *Theodore Roosevelt* (New York, 1931), 409.
15. Cited in Link, *The Struggle for Neutrality,* 383.

Lusitania controversy and continue the assault on neutral rights. In such case Wilson would have to break relations and probably take the country to war, or admit that his warnings and principles were meaningless. The latter was an intolerable course, as Wilson well knew, and yet he dreaded to put a threat in the form of a public diplomatic dispatch. He allowed Lansing to convey his thoughts privately to the German ambassador, Johann von Bernstorff: Germany must yield or face a diplomatic rupture.

The episode must have seemed for Bethmann an unfitting climax to a struggle he thought he had won. As the *Lusitania* controversy had continued into the summer, the chancellor had grown increasingly alarmed about relations with the United States. If he could see that Wilson was not going to war over the sinking, it was no less clear that the president intended to stand against the most severe features of submarine warfare. Bernstorff's cables from Washington had warned that despite Wilson's pacifist instincts, he had come dangerously close to a break with Germany. Bethmann became convinced that German-American relations could not withstand the sinking of another passenger ship, and yet under existing sailing instructions such an act was fully possible. To prevent that event, he insisted that the undersea fleet be given orders to avoid attacks on all passenger ships, even those vessels flying the enemy flag and possibly carrying contraband. The navy was furious. Not only had Tirpitz and Bachmann objected to concession on submarine warfare, they had demanded removal of previous guarantees for the safety of neutral ships, and the use of submarines without restriction. Faced with powerful military opposition, Bethmann had turned for support to another military man, the chief of the general staff, and the army leader had not disappointed him. Involved in a critical campaign in the Balkans, Falkenhayn could not understand how submarine warfare could provide much relief for his armies. He supported the chancellor's argument that nothing must be done to provoke the United States. In June orders had gone out that submarines were to avoid striking neutral ships and large passenger vessels. To prevent the appearance of a diplomatic defeat and an adverse public reaction, the instructions were kept secret.

For good reason, Bethmann was shocked to hear that a submarine had attacked the *Arabic,* a White Star liner of over fifteen thousand tons. Unable to learn the facts until the responsible submarine returned to base, which took several days, Bethmann felt that meanwhile he would have to do something to move the United States off its seemingly hostile course. It took another bitter dispute with the navy, continued support from Falkenhayn, and a conference with the kaiser before the chancellor won authority to grant all passenger ships immunity from sudden attack, and to make that position public. That promise was the so-called *Arabic* pledge, which Bernstorff submitted to Lansing on September 1. The government also secretly withdrew all submarines from the west coast of England and instructed commanders in the North Sea to operate only under rules of visit and search. Virtually a complete surrender on submarine warfare, these changes created a near crisis within the German government. For the admiral's zealous behavior, the kaiser dismissed Bachmann from his post, and when Tirpitz protested and extended his resignation, Wilhelm turned him down with an unusual show of strength: "America must be prevented from taking part against us as an active enemy. She could provide unlimited money for our foes. . . . As Chief Warlord, I had absolutely to prevent this event from occurring. . . . First the war must be won, and that end necessitates absolute protection against a new enemy; how that is to be achieved—whether with more or less sacrifice— is immaterial, and *my business.* What I do with my navy is my business *only.*" [16]

The *Arabic* pledge provided only momentary satisfaction for American officials. It was, of course, a very important concession—seemingly a means of avoiding the worst abuses of submarine warfare, and clear evidence of a diplomatic victory for Wilson. The German promise nonetheless pertained only

16. Cited in May, *The World War and American Isolation,* 223.

to future submarine procedure; it made no effort to settle the
case at hand, the *Arabic,* not to mention the *Lusitania.* There
arose in September a new furor inspired by delay in treating
the *Arabic* case and by widespread reports of blatant propaganda and spy activity in the United States. The latter led the
American government to demand the recall of the Austro-
Hungarian ambassador, Constantin Dumba, for his involvement, and Wilson was tempted to send Bernstorff home as
well.[17] The slowness in responding to charges about the
Arabic was largely attributable to difficulty in learning details
of the sinking on August 19. What in fact had happened was
that the submarine captain attacked the liner without recog-
nizing it as the *Arabic,* a passenger ship, or even a large vessel.
(But if the commander had identified the ship, he might have
fired anyway, for the admiralty had not yielded gracefully to
orders from the civil government. The order to spare large
liners was vague and allowed opportunity for convenient mistakes.) For some reason—probably at the instigation of superior naval officials—the commander falsified his report and
explained that he had acted out of retaliation, after the *Arabic*
tried to ram his craft. Though Bethmann believed this report,
he and his ambassador in Washington were so alarmed at the
prospect of a break in relations that they yielded everything
the United States demanded. Faced with vigilant and dramatic
pressure from Lansing, the beleaguered ambassador, partly
on his own initiative, repudiated the sinking of the *Arabic,*
promised an indemnity, and assured the United States that no
similar act could happen again.

While these concessions were a tribute to Wilson's patient,
persistent efforts to preserve neutral rights with measures short
of war—and at the time were so regarded—they would not
have been possible without help from the German chancellor.
Bethmann had risked a great deal, acting as he had: he had

17. The State Department obtained dispatches from the British
government which showed Dumba guilty of efforts to cripple American
munitions plants by inducing employees who were subjects of Austria-
Hungary to leave their jobs.

left naval officials seething with rage, opened his conduct to public disapproval, and weakened chances of stopping shipments of munitions and other supplies to the enemy. He made these decisions, as mentioned, primarily because of a realistic assessment of the effect American intervention would have on Germany's chances of winning. He also came to feel that a favorable settlement with Germany would inspire the United States to move with vigor against British encroachments on American neutral rights.

There certainly seemed reason for the United States to act against Britain in 1915. Armed with the blockade decree of March, the British navy had tightened the screws on trade destined for continental Europe. The subsequent sinking of the *Lusitania* and the focus of American policy on relations with Germany seemed to assure a virtual free hand in enforcement of the blockade. The United States had not exactly discouraged this activity, when one considers the outcome of the *Dacia* affair, the tone of the note of December 28, 1914, and Wilson's apparent acceptance of the blockade. In taking these positions, perhaps Wilson simply misunderstood British intention and assumed that a gentle response to the Order in Council of March 11 would encourage Britain to be considerate of American rights. It could be that the president wanted to allow Britain some leeway. It was still convenient to do so in March 1915, still advantageous to a general American prosperity and consistent with the president's view of the European war.

Whatever Wilson's purposes, events soon showed that he could not maintain the direction in which he had seemed headed in the spring. Public opinion reacted sharply to accelerated restrictions on trade, and some of the loudest protests came from newspapers or congressmen normally regarded as pro-British. Most irritating was Britain's large-scale seizure of cotton cargoes, an activity which again raised the specter of depression in the southern states. Ambassador Spring-Rice, admittedly an excitable man, filled his dispatches to Grey with warnings about an embargo on shipments of contraband to the Allies. And the sinking of the *Lusitania* was not in all respects beneficial to the Allies. This catastrophe doubtless delayed the sending of a sharp protest to Britain. Wilson and Lansing were preparing such a message when the ship went down. They did not send it until October. It also is true that the challenge of submarine warfare left American officials more than ever anxious to avoid serious dispute with the Allies. "In no event," the secretary of state had written House, "should we take a course that would seriously endanger our friendship with Great Britain, France, or Russia, for as you say, our friendship with Germany is a matter of the past." [18] At the same time the sinking of the *Lusitania,* and submarine warfare in general, inspired broader Allied maritime warfare and added to a generally dissatisfied American attitude toward all the major nations at war. Americans were tempted to conclude that one belligerent was almost as irritating as another, although Germany did use methods more drastic than Britain. Finally, the submarine crisis with Germany and Wilson's demands for strict observance of American rights left the need to press the Allies for observance no less strict. Bethmann's dispatches to Washington and Bernstorff's appeals to the secretary of state kept the American government reminded of what Germany expected of the United States, especially at times when Germany was willing to yield. Although Wilson insisted that he would deal with German relations apart from problems with the Allies, the record clearly shows that he recognized and respected the relationship.

Hence, during the summer of 1915, while the *Lusitania* negotiation was still in progress, the United States pestered the British government about detained ships, suggesting that Britain in many ways was going to have to do better. Walter Page painfully went over to the Foreign Office almost every day to talk about cases. He wrote House and Wilson that the United States was foolish, wrong, and damaging in what it was doing to Britain, and secretly searched for means to remove the sources of irritation. It was a difficult undertaking, inasmuch as any change would be costly to one government or the

18. July 30, 1915, House Papers.

other, and he was anxious to please both.

Grey also had a difficult time in the summer of 1915, for like the German chancellor he found himself between powerful opposing forces. Large sections of British opinion and several high officials, who felt that the United States dare not take action against the Allies, urged stronger measures, perhaps even a total blockade of northern and central Europe. Grey at the same time read opinion in the United States to mean that such activity would be legally indefensible, highly unpopular and too risky. The foreign secretary wished to press as far as possible. He believed that Wilson and most high American officials were favorable to the Allies, but he never could be sure. American policy had taken several twists, and Grey did not know what the president would do in the face of public and congressional protest.

The foreign secretary did act to remove one major source of irritation. As mentioned, cotton was useful in war material and probably eligible to be classified as contraband. Sound legal argument would have been of little practical value, however, had the placing of cotton on the contraband list (and subsequent seizure of this product) produced depression in the southern states and a crisis with the American government. After a series of complicated discussions—officially with cotton growers, and unofficially with members of the American government—Britain agreed to purchase large amounts of cotton to help maintain a decent market price. Thus armed against repercussion in the United States, Britain placed cotton on the contraband list on August 20, 1915, at a time when American opinion was aroused over the sinking of the *Arabic*. Surely one of the most effective acts of diplomacy during the entire period of American neutrality, this move would not have been possible had the British and Americans not developed a practice of peaceful cooperation in such difficult matters. The Germans in fact had offered an even better deal on cotton which the president, for reasons he did not feel compelled to explain, brushed aside.

The cotton arrangement did not clear up all issues, and

through the summer and fall of 1915 the United States continued to complain about violations of neutral rights. Grey continued to muddle along, looking for clues for distinguishing safe policy from unsafe. Time after time he pled his case before Ambassador Page: that it was absolutely essential for the Allies to keep supplies from reaching Germany, and that if Britain granted all American demands about neutral rights, he might as well "throw up the sponge," and give up all effort to blockade the enemy. Did the United States wish to impose this burden on the Allies, and help Germany win the war? Page of course answered no, and tried to assure his British friend that the situation was not as bad as it seemed, but the ambassador was hard pressed to explain why the State Department continued to "nag" about this or that aspect of British maritime warfare. The foreign secretary was so distressed that at one stage (in July 1915) he was prepared to urge his government to give up the quasi-blockade and fall back on rules of contraband. The precise effect of such a change is difficult to measure, but beyond doubt the Allies thereupon would have relinquished some restriction on trade with Germany. Grey knew it would have been a costly act—in supplies going to the enemy and in its unpopularity with British and Allied opinion; he nonetheless was prepared to absorb these penalties rather than risk retaliation from the United States.

As it turned out Britain never found it necessary to revise the structure or reduce the impact of maritime warfare, which meant that British officials did not find American opinion aroused enough to demand a change. The United States in October sent another formal protest. That action was no surprise. German concessions on submarine warfare had made it virtually inevitable, and the president had been contemplating such a move since May. Yet the message emerged in a fashion relaxed and leisurely compared with the urgent treatment given the submarine question. The world to Wilson seemed much brighter after Germany yielded on the *Arabic,* and it probably is not too much to say that German concessions had made the whole matter of neutral rights less bothersome.

The president left the preparation of the note to Lansing and his associates, adding only a touch here and there.

From all appearances the note was strong. A detailed, legalistic document, it surveyed all major aspects of the British quasi-blockade, challenged many features as illegal, pointed out those practices which were costly and in violation of American neutral rights. It emphatically protested interference with American produce consigned to neutral countries and the seemingly endless delay in dealing with ships brought to port, and reiterated the American government's intent to press for the fullest expression of neutral rights. If the purpose of the message was to appease American and German opinion —these sensitivities actually had inspired the note—it was a success. Editorial comment was favorable in Germany and the United States. Bernstorff was delighted, the British press angry. Page, on reading the massive paper, called it "an uncourteous monster of 35 heads and 3 appendices." [19] If the purpose of the note was to force a radical change, it was a failure. Amidst the maze of legal argument there appeared no threat or possibility of reprisal, no hint of what the United States might do if Britain continued its vexing ways. Perhaps more important than sending a formal note is the way officials handle their government's case in informal discussion. Lansing had spoken so strongly to Bernstorff that the ambassador had placed his post in jeopardy to meet the American demands. The secretary of state gave no similar performance with Spring-Rice. Intentionally or not, Lansing let word leak out that the United States did not plan to give Britain trouble. The note, he confidentially told an American newspaperman, "was a political safety valve, [and] not much was expected of it, as it would certainly not be pressed." [20] The newsman, Frederick Dixon of the *Boston Monitor,* sent an account of the interview to Lord Robert Cecil, British undersecretary, who accepted it as an accurate statement of American policy, consistent with unof-

19. Hendrick, *Page,* II, 78.
20. Frederick Dixon to Lord Robert Cecil, undated (stamped Nov. 10, 1915), Foreign Office Papers, 382/12.

ficial reports he had heard from other Americans. Cecil and other Foreign Office personnel agreed that Britain safely could stand on all important aspects of the blockade. When near the end of the year Spring-Rice again raised the possibility of embargo, the Foreign Office made preparation for a retaliatory response which would involve cutting off—or threatening to cut off—shipments to the United States of raw material from Allied nations and their colonies.

Ignorant of the stiffening attitude within the British Foreign Office, President Wilson could experience a great deal of satisfaction as 1915 came to an end. When one considers the terrible problems of the previous months it seems almost unbelievable that the nation could have maintained the position it held at the end of the year. Wilson—as he had pledged himself to do—had preserved peace with honor. He had forced major concessions from the German government and seemingly removed the major source of trouble. He had pleased public opinion with a detailed expression of unwillingness to accept the British blockade, all while pursuing, at least to his satisfaction, an impartial course.

It was what the president did not know that would prove most troublesome. To be sure, Wilson had not deceived himself into thinking that neutrality hereafter would be easy, but he did not know, for example, the great difficulty Bethmann had endured to give Wilson his victory, the problems the German chancellor would face holding the military in line. Sending a note to Britain was a popular and seemingly impartial act, but what if Britain chose to ignore the questions raised in the message? Wilson did not know of Grey's lessened influence in the British government, the growing strength of those officials who felt that Britain could do virtually as it wished and the United States would dare not resist. Perhaps Wilson never would learn the full details about inner workings of the belligerent governments. The outcome of their deliberations he soon enough would discover.

4

Months of Trouble
and Reprieve

SUCCESSFUL as American wartime policy had been in 1915, neither Wilson nor any other public official allowed himself to think that problems of neutrality were gone. Each belligerent had shown itself guided by reasons of self-interest and not the legal and moral principles to which Wilson had appealed. Administration officials realized, for example, that if the Germans had yielded out of expediency on the submarine issue, they soon might find it practical to withdraw the concessions. The other side offered little more hope, and by early 1916, several weeks after the last American note, there was no evidence that the British government felt it necessary to grant concessions on matters of trade. Judging by editorials in British newspapers, it seemed fully possible that Britain would place even more restrictions on American commerce. Hence, the problems of submarine and blockade, when not pressing on the minds and nerves of American policy makers, were hovering about, always on the verge of a new crisis.

American opinion, moreover, continued to be difficult to judge and almost impossible to please. Taken as a whole, opinion had not changed much in the final months of 1915. Still more pro-Ally than pro-German, Americans continued to expect their government to uphold rights and honor, keep open the trade lanes to Europe, and preserve peace for the United States. At the same time, pressure groups were ever willing to make their views known, ever watchful for policy which seemed contrary to their wishes. While the president insisted he would conduct diplomacy on its merits, he could not forget that 1916 was a presidential election year.

Faced with these conflicting forces, the president and his advisers undertook in the final days of 1915 and first weeks of 1916 a bewildering series of diplomatic moves. Wilson and Lansing first sought to assure the public that the administration upheld national honor and left the nation able to defend itself. These steps involved the modest preparedness campaign of 1915–16, a rigid response to new submarine sinkings (none of which, as it turned out, violated German pledges), and more pressure for settlement of the *Lusitania* issue. The last two moves brought the nation close to a break with Germany and Austria-Hungary. The administration at the same time reminded such pacifists as Bryan that the object was peace, and a little later had to fight off an attempt in Congress to keep Americans off belligerent ships. Meanwhile Colonel House departed for a new journey to Europe, a mission that on one hand offered the prospect of a mediated peace, and on the other, if the first plan did not work, the possibility of intervention on the side of the Allies. While House attempted to induce the British to agree to mediation or some other scheme, Lansing set forth a plan to have the Allies disarm merchant vessels, in return for Germany's stopping submarine warfare. These moves came partly as a response to new problems placed before the government, partly as an attempt to devise new policies that would remove old problems, partly as an effort to appease those American groups that made the most noise. Confusing and sometimes contradictory, the moves would have aroused sharp public criticism had not some of the activity taken place in secret. Together, these attempts suggest the difficulty of upholding peace, honor, and commercial rights. And after they had run their course, the United States faced nothing less than a new submarine crisis.

Though the least known at the time, the House scheme

was the most ambitious American proposal of 1916 and offered the most decisive turn in diplomacy. Thoughts of mediation rarely left Wilson's mind, not only because he thought it the humane thing to do, but because he came to realize that peace in Europe was the only way to keep the United States out of the war. He had extended American good offices at the outbreak of war in 1914, had sent House to Europe searching for feelers in the spring of 1915, and in general stood ready to seize upon anything that remotely resembled an opening for mediation. No such opening had appeared, and while Wilson could rejoice at diplomatic victories gained in the latter part of 1915, he knew that neutrality was more hazardous and far less certain at the end of the year than at the beginning.

Nothing would have pleased House more than to promote a major change in the course of the war and American neutrality. A soft-spoken, almost secretive little man with a small, neatly-trimmed mustache, thin, tight lips, and long, narrow face, House liked being the mystery man of the Wilson administration. The contrast between his diminutive features, quiet manner, and rumored great political strength was too obvious not to point out. House took pleasure in telling nothing to reporters who followed him about—a silence which suggested, whether true or not, that the Colonel had information too important to be made public. This is not to suggest that House undertook his activity primarily for purposes of self-glorification, but, as his diary suggests, he took pleasure in the aura of drama and intrigue which followed where he went.

House above all was concerned that American policy, instead of following a positive course, was no more than a conglomeration of responses to problems, the continuance of which would keep the nation in endless difficulty and end eventually in war. It seemed neither fitting nor wise that a great nation should leave its fate to other countries, and so in late 1915 he devised a scheme to allow the United States to shape its destiny. House suggested that he travel to belligerent capitals, probe the feeling about mediation, and say that Wilson was anxious to guide a peace settlement. By telling each side that the other likely would refuse American peace terms, he might be able to bring the nations to agreement without their knowing it. If Germany refused Wilson's peace terms and the Allies accepted, the United States would enter the war on the side of the Allies. Wilson enthusiastically endorsed the plan and the mission, hoping they might become the vehicle for avoiding American intervention. His sole reservation was to qualify House's second alternative: if Germany refused to make peace, the United States "probably" would enter the war. He did not want a final commitment.

Arriving in Britain on January 5, 1916, House spent a few days in London, traveled for conferences in Berlin, stopped for a short time in Paris on the way back, returned to London on February 9. As usual, reporters collected at stopping places all along the line, and House was his usual talkative self. Witness the interview in London on February 10:

"Did you hear any discussion on the possibilities of peace?" a reporter asked.

"I have not heard peace discussions anywhere because I purposely avoided them," House answered.

"Did you see any signs of a shortage of bread in Germany?"— "I did not see any signs of anything in particular." . . .

"You will report to the Senate on your return?"—"I do not know what I shall do. I may have nothing to report." . . .

"Did you find the Berlin people very cheerful?"—"I made no inquiries of any kind. I did not make any observation of any kind." . . .

"Did you form any impression as to how long the war will last?"—"Not the slightest." . . .

"But there was a good deal that interested you?"—"Europe is always interesting." . . .

House at last did give one direct answer. "Are they having nice fine weather in Berlin?" a reporter asked, almost out of exasperation. "Yes," answered House. "I found the weather very mild everywhere." [1]

Officials in all countries, if sometimes noncommittal, treated House with courtesy and respect, the sort of dealing

1. Seymour, *The Intimate Papers of Colonel House,* II, 187.

which reflected an understanding of House's close relation with the president. The only exception was Page, who was almost beside himself—as House put it, like a "petulant woman"—out of opposition to House's plan or any proposal pointed toward ending the war before an Allied victory. Page was unceasingly critical of the State Department's short-sighted, "nagging" policy, in one diatribe half-seriously suggesting that the Department be "cleaned out from top to bottom," starting by taking "a large tent and [placing] it on the green near the Washington Monument in order to raze the present building to its foundations and start afresh with new surroundings and a new force." [2] "I wish he could go home for a while," noted House out of weariness and irritation.[3] The Colonel did his best to ignore Page and proceed approximately as planned: in Berlin he raised the general question of mediation, implying that British officials had not seemed favorable. From discussion he decided that the Germans were not ready for peace talks, a conclusion he did not find exactly displeasing. In Paris and London the tone was different. House told French officials that Wilson sought a peace favorable to the Allies, that the United States likely would be at war with Germany before the end of the year. In London also, House was free with expressions of sympathy for the Allies and with the opinion that the United States soon would take part in the conflict. He did lay his formal proposal before British leaders. Known as the House-Grey memorandum, the plan was set down as follows by the foreign secretary:

Colonel House told me that President Wilson was ready, on hearing from France and England that the moment was opportune, to propose that a conference should be summoned to put an end to the war. Should the Allies accept this proposal, and should Germany refuse it, the United States would probably enter the war against Germany.

Colonel House expressed the opinion that if such a conference met, it would secure peace on terms not unfavorable to the Allies; and if it failed to secure peace, the United States would leave the

2. House Diary, February 10, 1916.
3. *Ibid.*, January 12, 1916.

conference as a belligerent on the side of the Allies, if Germany
was unreasonable.[4]

House returned to the United States thinking that the British
were in full agreement and would select the time for Wilson
to act.

Thus the House peace plan, which began, at least to Wilson's thinking, as a means of bringing the war to a negotiated
end, had become at the time of its presentation largely a device for promoting American intervention on the side of the
Allies. The Colonel would have been pleased had a successful
peace conference grown out of his discussions in Europe; he
would have been delighted to know he had brought it about.
He nonetheless became convinced from travel in belligerent
capitals that such a conference was a virtual impossibility—
that Germany would not submit to conditions the Allies would
demand, many of which House also would have liked to see
incorporated into a permanent settlement. The Colonel let
these thoughts be known to officials in Paris and London. Unaware of the promises House had scattered about Europe, Wilson was delighted to see his little friend return to the United
States after planting, as the president saw it, seeds for a lasting
peace. Perhaps the most curious aspect of the episode was that
House expressed no concern, either in his diary or in any other
place, over the way he had been deceiving—or at least misleading—Wilson, not even an indication he knew he was doing so.

As it turned out, House's activity in Europe was a wasted
effort, for British officials never could bring themselves to ask
Wilson to act. If the United States indeed was interested in
mediation, the Allies wanted no part of the plan. An inconclusive peace was no fit ending for such a ghastly and costly
struggle, and officials in Britain and France believed that a
continuance of the conflict would lead to victory. House in fact
had confessed that peace discussion "would be about as popular in England as the coronation of the Kaiser in Westminster

4. Grey, *Twenty-five Years*, II, 127–28.

Abbey." [5] Of course a fear of mediation would have been superfluous had Allied leaders taken House's promises at face value. One is left with the conclusion that Grey, Prime Minister Herbert Asquith, and other officials either did not believe House or did not believe he represented the thoughts of Wilson. From the Allied point of view, one might summarize the situation as follows: House had asserted that Wilson was willing, even anxious, to promote American intervention. Yet he would not act through a straightforward declaration of war, the procedure Grey once told House would be best. Events soon showed that the president would not act even after Germany had provoked a new crisis over submarine warfare. Wilson would move only after the ritual of proposing a conference which House promised was all but doomed to failure. It sounded too complicated to be believable. British leaders never placed faith in House's proposal; they patronized the Colonel, at times even showed him enthusiasm, for fear of antagonizing the American government.

Even so, the British would have to suffer for rejecting this proposal they did not fully understand. Failure to encourage mediation led Wilson to question whether Britain was fighting for the high moral purposes it had claimed. The proposal accentuated other diplomatic difficulty and, before the end of 1916, contributed to bringing Anglo-American relations to their lowest point of the war.

If the British were skeptical of the House peace plan, they were astonished at another American diplomatic maneuver that came at about the same time. Secretary Lansing proposed on January 18—House at the time was in the midst of his European travels—that the Allies remove all guns from merchant vessels as the first step toward German renunciation of submarine warfare. Lansing reasoned that if submarine commanders knew merchant vessels were unarmed—incapable of firing on a surfaced U-boat—they would have no objection to stopping them on the sea, and that the Allies would grant this

5. Seymour, *The Intimate Papers of Colonel House*, II, 184.

concession to obtain security against sudden submarine attacks. The secretary of state saw such slight distinction between a cruiser and armed merchant ship (blockade cruisers after all were only merchantmen with guns on them) that he questioned whether the latter vessels deserved the privileges the United States customarily had granted noncombatant ships in American ports. Behind these thoughts was the happy prospect of Americans and American ships traveling the sea free of submarine harassment and its entangling consequences.

More honest and certainly simpler than House's plan, the Lansing proposal left the impression in Britain that one hand of the administration did not know what the other was doing, though presumably the president was guiding both. It was contradictory to House's babbling in London and Paris about American eagerness to intervene in the war. Given a choice of two American policies, the British and French took Lansing's plan as the more believable and consistent with goals Wilson had described for the United States.

The Allies obtained no pleasure from this choice, for they regarded the armed merchantman proposal as unfair and possibly dangerous. As the Allies saw it, they were being asked to relinquish practices grounded in law and precedent (the right to arm merchantmen long had been recognized by international law) in return for Germany's abandoning rights it did not have. The proposal suggested that the United States not only was prepared to recognize submarine warfare as legitimate, but was asking the Allies—by agreeing to bargain—also to recognize it. The most frightful aspect of Lansing's message was the possibility that it represented a bargain with Germany. Spring-Rice had warned that recent German-American discussion about the sinking of the *Lusitania* might soon reach a successful conclusion. He reported a conversation with Lansing on January 13, 1916, in which the secretary had said that Germany and the United States probably would reach agreement on all outstanding issues. The Lansing proposal, coming only five days later, seemed clear evidence that Germany had granted all the United States had asked on the issue of the

Lusitania in return for a promise to press the Allies in matters of blockade and armed merchantmen. Virtually every official in the British Foreign Office privately expressed extreme irritation at the American proposition. Grey behaved somewhat differently. It was not his style to harangue and threaten the United States, but he did look pained and sorrowful before Walter Page, and he instructed Spring-Rice to express in Washington his feeling of "disappointment and dismay." [6]

Faced with the discouraging positions of Grey and Spring-Rice; the sharp, almost threatening cables of Walter Page; and the fact that the Allies would not accept the Lansing plan unless forced to do so, the State Department had no choice but to withdraw. Although Lansing felt the proposal fair and acceptable on its merits, he had no intention of forcing it on Britain, possibly causing the sort of trouble it was to prevent. The secretary announced on February 15, 1916, that the United States would neither insist upon the *modus vivendi* nor treat armed merchantmen as cruisers.

Even though Lansing's statement quieted rumblings in London, albeit after placing a new strain on British-American relations, it did not end all controversy involving the question of armed merchantmen. The secretary's maneuver unwittingly had helped open doors he and the president preferred to keep closed. In explaining his proposal to the Central Powers, Lansing had repeated his belief that placing guns on merchant ships perhaps changed their character. He went so far as to tell the Austro-Hungarian representative on January 26 that he would welcome an announcement that submarines would treat armed merchantmen as auxiliary cruisers (Lansing later denied using the word "welcome"). In Berlin, Chancellor Bethmann was delighted to receive this news, for it seemed a way to avoid a new struggle with naval officials, who by this time were squirming with impatience to turn the submarines loose. In any event, Bethmann probably would have had to make some concession to the navy, but it now seemed possible to act without provok-

6. The foreign secretary to Ambassador Spring-Rice, Jan. 25, 1916, Foreign Office Papers, 382/929.

ing a crisis with the United States. Thus on February 10, the German government informed the State Department that submarines after February 29 would renew warfare against armed enemy freighters.

By the time the message arrived in the American capital, opinion had changed. Lansing and Wilson now understood the futility and perhaps the impracticality of pressing the armed-ship *modus vivendi*. Wilson was particularly concerned that it might weaken House's negotiations in Europe. It also was necessary to reassess an earlier inclination toward reclassification of freighters with guns on them. Lansing now was in the uncomfortable position of having to reject—at least not accept— German policy he had helped inspire. Speaking to reporters on February 15, he did the best he could: he said that while he still believed merchantmen should not carry guns, the United States would not insist on the proposed *modus vivendi* and would not classify armed freighters as cruisers. The secretary then made an unconvincing distinction between offensive and defensive armament: a merchantman with armament superior to that of a submarine probably was armed offensively. Submarine attacks on a defensively armed vessel with Americans aboard would be serious for German-American relations. It was not a bad effort, considering the corner into which Lansing had backed himself. The statement nonetheless pointed to great problems of submarine warfare. It was difficult to determine when a vessel had offensive or defensive armament, even if Germany accepted that distinction. In view of the handicap under which submarines operated, it was difficult to discover if a ship was armed at all. The upshot of the episode was that it increased the likelihood of those events Lansing had designed the armed-ship proposal to prevent.

A result of the German submarine pronouncement was to bring an unsuccessful end to negotiation over the sinking of the *Lusitania*. Lansing and Bernstorff had engaged in intermittent discussion of this matter for several weeks, during which the secretary of state exploited new events—the sinking in November 1915 of the Italian liner *Ancona,* and the revelation of German spy activity—to press a hard line on the German ambassador. On January 25 he gloomily had spoken of a break in relations. The German government was prepared to express regret for the loss of American lives and offer an indemnity, in "a spirit of friendship and conciliation," not out of a feeling of obligation.[7] It would not concede that the sinking was illegal or unjustified. Unwilling at first to accept the German offer, Wilson and Lansing concluded in the face of new events—particularly, what seemed to be the success of the House mission—that the United States should not press Germany further, and that the settlement was the best they could obtain. The United States almost had accepted the German offer when there came on February 10 the announcement of the new campaign against armed merchant ships. Lansing informed Bernstorff that because of these recent developments the United States could not accept the proposed settlement. The issue of the *Lusitania,* like the great Cunard liner itself, was therefore at rest, left unresolved, never to be resurrected during the course of the war.

Finally, the confusing events of January and February 1916 inspired a revolt in Congress which threatened the standards Wilson had set for American neutrality and for the president's authority to control foreign policy. The president and secretary of state were partly to blame for this disturbance; their juggling the status of armed merchantmen provoked a reaction from congressmen unwilling to change directions so fast. When Lansing had offered his proposal of January 18, he had said that armed merchant ships were virtually the same as warships. Hastening to agree, Germany had proclaimed on February 10 that submarines would attack such vessels without warning. Five days later Lansing announced cancellation of his proposal, and on February 21 the president pledged to a group of congressmen his intent to defend the right of Americans to travel on merchant vessels even if the ships were armed, though he did make the unclear distinction between offensive and defensive armament that Lansing earlier had

7. *The Lansing Papers,* I, 519–20.

mentioned. Wilson said that he would break relations if a German submarine sank an armed merchant ship with Americans aboard. To some people it seemed that the administration was almost asserting the right to travel unmolested on belligerent warships, a totally unreasonable claim, unparalleled in the history of warfare. It seemed equally certain that the president's policy, coupled with the German pronouncement of February 10, had placed the nations on a course that would end in war.

What resulted were the so-called Gore-McLemore resolutions (one was offered in the House, the other in the Senate), which—by keeping Americans off armed merchant vessels, or ships carrying contraband, or both—meant to avoid any incident that might lead to war. The followers of Bryan expressed expected enthusiasm for these measures, and a good many Democrats from whom the president ordinarily could expect support also indicated their willingness to vote for one resolution or the other. Seized by sudden fear that Wilson in fact desired intervention, supporters of the movement built such momentum that at one stage it seemed the resolutions would pass by overwhelming majorities.

The proposals are of considerable interest, for they aroused the strongest sentiment the nation had shown for turning away from Wilson's standards of neutrality. Even so, they do not offer a clear indication of the wishes of the people, or even of Congress. Because the measures never passed, one cannot know their final form, or what restrictions they would have placed on neutral rights. The movement grew out of a state of panic; many congressmen had concluded that war was almost certain, and they were desperate to head it off. The proposals seemed to say that, faced with a simple decision of war or peace, a large number of people would choose peace, and they saw no need to look beyond that conclusion. If there would have followed a cumulative abandonment of maritime rights and privileges, as Wilson feared, it is by no means certain the nation would have been satisfied with its course. The rapidity with which support was to dwindle suggested a lack of depth and conviction in the movement. It also suggested that the nation wanted peace and neutral rights if it could see a decent chance for having both.

Wilson would have no part of the proposals, for he regarded them as disruptive of the policy he had planned for the United States. He was particularly concerned that an intrusion into presidential authority in foreign relations would weaken the efforts to bring the warring powers to a peace conference. The president had the highest hopes that House, now winding up the European visit, would return with plans for quick implementation of the mediation proposal. He moved to quash the rebellion in Congress, choosing as a device a letter written February 24 to Senator William J. Stone, chairman of the Foreign Relations Committee, and released for publication the next day. After reiterating his intent to keep the nation out of war, Wilson entered into a vigorous defense of American honor, saying he would accept not "a single abatement of right" or violation of international law.[8] While the president did not mention the matter of Americans traveling on armed merchant ships, he left the impression that this right, no less than any other, must be left untouched. Persons unsettled over this question found little satisfaction in the statement. Faced with an impending clash over submarine warfare, Wilson seemed to say only that Germany must yield. The letter nonetheless suited its purpose: it served notice that he intended to control foreign policy, that congressmen, and particularly Democrats, who wished to encroach upon this authority would have to deal with the president. The number of insurgent congressmen dwindled rapidly, particularly after Lansing explained that the administration would support the right of Americans to travel on ships armed only for defense. Representative McLemore said that he would not press a vote on his resolution, at least not yet. Upon the president's urging, both houses eventually (in March) did act on the measures, giving each a decisive defeat.

8. *New York Times,* Feb. 26, 1916; see also Arthur S. Link, *Wilson: Confusions and Crises, 1915–1916* (Princeton, N. J., 1964), 170–78.

It had been an active, confusing, and at the same time futile two months of diplomatic maneuver. Much of the confusion stemmed from the fact that Wilson temporarily had
allowed management of policy to slip from his hands. Such was
true of the House mission, although it is difficult to explain how
Wilson could have exerted closer control over his friend. For
clarity and continuity of policy, it would have been better had
House stayed in the United States. The armed-merchant-ship
proposal with its troublesome ramifications was essentially
Lansing's work. While the president approved the plan and
thus showed no more foresight than his secretary of state, he
did not give the proposal the attention it deserved. The futility
of these two months of diplomacy was perhaps ordained, if
one considers that it asked little of the United States and a
great deal of the belligerents. The United States in each case
had proposed to change not American policy but the policy of
the nations at war. The failure of the Europeans to respond is
understandable, since the Americans offered no great reward
(House's unconvincing promises in London to the contrary)
and threatened no punishment if they did or did not comply.
The president was left with the obligation of holding up both
ends of his great dilemma—the preservation of American
honor, which in his interpretation involved a broad range of
rights and privileges, and keeping the nation at peace. One or
the other goal was obtainable if the nation was willing to exert
the necessary effort. To obtain both became steadily more
difficult.

The diplomacy of January and February 1916 in fact had
worsened Wilson's tasks, for he now was committed to protecting travel on armed merchant ships, a question previously
untouched, and the United States faced the prospect of a new
submarine campaign. Efforts to distinguish between defensive
and offensive armament had helped matters not at all. No one
had attempted to determine how many guns would constitute
offensive arming. Britain said that none of its vessels had arms
for anything but defense. The German government gave orders for submarines to attack all armed vessels. The United

States inevitably faced a dispute, if not a crisis, over the question of submarines and armed merchantmen. When the incident finally took place it fortunately involved a ship that carried no guns.

On March 24, 1916, a submarine attacked the *Sussex,* a channel steamer of French registry. It was the sort of event Wilson had said was intolerable. The vessel carried passengers and was unarmed, and even though it did not sink, some eighty persons died as a result of the torpedo explosion. Of the twenty-five or so Americans aboard, none lost their lives, but four received injury. In striking the *Sussex* the submarine commander had violated the spirit of his government's pledges to the United States and the letter of instructions from the admiralty. At the same time it was not totally a mistake, and certainly no accident, for naval officials, frustrated after many weeks of inactivity, were not diligent in assuring that U-boat commanders observe strict adherence to the government's wishes, and the commanders bound themselves to no meticulous identification of the vessels sighted in their periscopes. The commander of the *U-29* thought the *Sussex* was a minelayer, although he was not sure what it was and did not much care.

In this time of crisis Wilson moved to take personal charge, and not, as had happened in previous weeks, allow others to propose policy he had not thought out. He was deliberate, even slow, in responding. He occasionally discussed the attack with Lansing and House, but much of the time shut himself off from virtually everyone and even left Washington for a long weekend cruise. Associates took these familiar signs to mean that the president was procrastinating, and would not act. House noted on April 2: "Grayson [Wilson's physician] thinks the President is a man of unusually narrow prejudices and is intolerant of advice. I did not argue the matter with him as I feel that while the President is not unwilling to accept advice from me, Grayson's general characterization of him is correct. Grayson says if one urges Wilson to do something contrary to his own conviction, he ceases to have any liking for that person.

He does not like to meet people and isolates himself as much as anyone I have ever known. His immediate entourage, from the Secretary of State down, are having an unhappy time just now. He is consulting none of them and they are as ignorant of his intentions as the man in the street." [9]

Wilson's policy had narrowed the alternatives now before him. Failure to respond, or a weak response, was unthinkable —contrary to the standards he had set for the United States, humiliating for the president, not to mention the danger of encouraging the opening of unlimited submarine warfare. His handling of the *Arabic* incident had made a worn-out technique of an informal private threat. The president saw but two choices: to break relations or threaten a breach pending German willingness to grant everything the United States demanded. The first response, which House and Lansing favored, would have constituted public admission that war was unavoidable and wise. A threat to break relations—ordinarily a stern and rigid posture—was in these circumstances the moderate course. In choosing the latter Wilson was expressing hope that there still was a chance to keep the nation at peace.

The *Sussex* note, dispatched on April 18, was nonetheless no conciliatory message. It carried a denunciation of the attack on the *Sussex* and of submarine warfare in general. Abandoning all effort to distinguish between defensively and offensively armed merchantmen, the note threatened that if Germany did not "abandon its present method of submarine warfare against passenger and freight-carrying vessels," the United States would break diplomatic relations.[10] The president at last had come to the position he had struggled to avoid for nearly a year.

If the American threat brought sharpened tension to the German government, the task of resolving the issue was not as difficult as might be expected, for in the weeks before the sink-

9. *House Diary,* April 2, 1916.
10. The secretary of state to Ambassador Gerard, April 18, 1916, *Papers Relating to the Foreign Relations of the United States, 1916, Supplement* (Washington, D.C., 1929), 232–34.

ing took place, Bethmann had successfully refought the submarine issue. The conflict had begun anew in January 1916 when the chancellor faced from seemingly all sides a movement for resumption of unrestricted submarine warfare. Public opinion strongly supported the move. The leaders of German opinion, not understanding the intricacies of diplomatic calculation, could see only that the government had truckled to the United States, and was standing in way of victories the navy promised it could provide.

Naval spokesmen were assisted by the publicity given the *Baralong* case, a submarine incident which had taken place several weeks earlier. A submarine had stopped a British merchantman in the Irish Sea, and the commander was dutifully waiting for the passengers to disembark when there appeared a steamer flying the American flag and carrying red, white, and blue markings. The vessel was in fact the *Baralong,* a British decoy ship. As it approached within a hundred yards the ship suddenly hoisted the British flag, fired, and quickly sank the U-Boat. The *Baralong's* crew then turned on German seamen floundering in the water and brutally shot as many as were within sight. If the episode shocked Wilson and Lansing, one can imagine the effect on German opinion when the news became public in January 1916. The *Baralong* case not merely exposed British treachery and aroused cries for reprisal, it suggested the danger of using submarines under rules of visit and search.

Tirpitz and his followers then made every effort to exploit what seemed to be a favorable climate of opinion. They mustered a huge press campaign from newsmen who agreed with their views. They petitioned the kaiser, members of the legislature, and the army for a resumption of unlimited submarine warfare, arguing that the submarines could win the war, that a campaign of six to eight months would lessen supplies going to Allied armies and destroy Britain's ability to continue. Tirpitz seemingly gained a major victory when he won support of the chief of the general staff, Falkenhayn. The army leader never had been comfortable supporting the civil government against his military confederate, and he became convinced that a submarine campaign would benefit his armies then preparing a massive assault on the French fortress at Verdun. Faced with what seemed overwhelming domestic forces, and encouraged by Lansing's clumsy handling of the armed ship proposal, Bethmann had yielded to allow submarines to attack merchant ships in the war zone. But the admirals were not satisfied. Determined to have nothing less than an unrestricted campaign, the navy forced a showdown over submarine warfare.

In the contest which followed, the chancellor gave a splendid display of political maneuver. He charged that the navy did not have as many submarines available for duty as claimed (Tirpitz had said there were at least a hundred), and doubted if submarines could disable the British merchant fleet. He re-emphasized the detrimental effect American intervention would have on the war—the huge contribution the United States could make in supplies, money, and eventually in manpower—and argued that other neutral European nations probably would follow the United States into the conflict. In short, American intervention would prolong indefinitely the ability of the Allies to resist, would destroy the possibility of a German victory, and would greatly multiply the chances of defeat. In a clever appeal to the kaiser's vanity, Bethmann made it appear that Tirpitz and supporters, in attacking government decisions, were criticizing the emperor and perhaps challenging the principle of monarchy. Finally, he announced that if the navy resumed submarine warfare he would resign. It was a presentation so convincing that the kaiser, as always wavering from one decision to another, refused to overrule the chancellor. Sensing his strengthened position, Bethmann then moved to get rid of his major military rival. He maneuvered a minor change in the executive department which he knew Tirpitz would resist. Taking the bait, the proud old sea dog offered his resignation, and Wilhelm accepted it.

The decision on the *Sussex,* coming shortly after this series of conferences, was not difficult. Inasmuch as the chancellor had challenged the usefulness of submarine warfare, and pointed to the danger of American intervention, there seemed nothing to do but yield to the United States. With Tirpitz silenced, if not discredited, the admirals offered no vigorous objection to following Bethmann's lead.

The American government on May 4 received a formal reply to the *Sussex* note. The United States hardly could have asked for more. The note conceded that the attack on the *Sussex* had been wrong and said that the guilty submarine commander had received punishment. Most important was the promise that submarines would operate only under rules of visit and search. There was to be no "submarine warfare," only submarines acting as cruisers. The Germans did leave themselves one loophole. The note concluded by saying that if the United States in return did not compel Britain to observe international law, the German government reserved its liberty of decision.

Though the effort to make the concession dependent upon British policy was unacceptable, and Wilson conveyed this message to Berlin, the note in other respects was gratifying and promising. It reaffirmed Wilson's delicate efforts to uphold neutral rights and honor, and allowed the danger of war to pass, at least for a while. It enhanced the president's prestige as a world leader, strengthened his position as chief executive and leader of American foreign relations. It also provided leverage when he undertook the campaign for re-election.

One point must be made about Wilson's handling of relations with Germany: he never took victories for more than they were. It was no mean accomplishment to force the German government to retreat, as Wilson had done. Yet while the president doubtless enjoyed the praise American newspapers heaped on him, he allowed no boasting about the settlement of the *Sussex* crisis, nor did he overestimate his ability to influence German policy. He correctly saw the German concession as an expedient diplomatic maneuver in effect only until it became expedient to change. In the period following the *Sussex* settlement Wilson set to work on other aspects of diplomacy, hoping to rearrange conditions so as to make a future submarine campaign unnecessary. This activity led to a sharpening of tension in British relations and new efforts toward a mediated peace.

Picking a quarrel with Britain was no task at all, for while the United States had been embroiled with Germany the British in their quiet manner had been busy finding ways to interrupt any American activity which might prove beneficial to the enemy. This behavior alone would have justified resurrecting old disputes with Britain and France. The *Sussex* crisis had made action all the more necessary. It had left Wilson more committed than ever to observance of international law, and if for no other reasons than to remain consistent and satisfy personal honesty, the president would have had to direct some of these principles at the Allies.

Not the least irritating feature of new measures of trade restrictions was that they came despite the vigorous American protest of November 1915, so close in fact as to suggest to Americans—what was true—that Britain did not take the American note seriously. The accelerated activity came partly as a result of French pressure at an Allied War Council in January 1916, partly as a result of British public opinion which had come to believe that during a struggle for national survival, their government was coddling the Americans. Any such activity had to be based on a calculation that the United States would not reply in any harmful way. As one member of the House of Lords advised the government: "Americans do not love us and will not actively help us—indeed, being an undisciplined democracy, they will often say nasty things to us—but as a matter of fact they want us to win and they expect us to 'play up.' " [11] While most Britons probably held this view of the United States, the Foreign Office was more impressed by the economic relationship which had grown up between the two nations, the fact that measures Wilson might use in retaliation—such as an embargo—would be almost as harmful to Americans as to the British. Grey was less certain of this conclusion than others in the government, but his influence was

11. Memorandum, Jan. 24, 1916, by Lord Eustace Percy, Grey Papers.

not what it once had been and rumors were circulating that he was on his way out. Early in 1916 the cabinet created a new post, minister of blockade, and placed at its head Lord Robert Cecil, an advocate of stringent economic warfare. While Cecil technically remained subordinate to Grey, he began to perform many functions the foreign secretary once had managed. Grey then actively promoted, or allowed to take place, such policy as the interception of a large number of ships headed for continental Europe and inspection of almost every piece of correspondence sent from the United States to persons in European countries, whether neutral or belligerent. Not until April 1916 did Britain answer the American note sent in October 1915, and the answer was unsatisfactory.

In one way, trouble with the United States was not of Britain's making, for in the spring of 1916 Grey had to ward off efforts to resurrect the House mediation scheme. The British and French, of course, had dismissed the plan almost as soon as they heard it, although House and Wilson had not understood that fact. Pampered and misled in London, House came home to await Grey's signal for Wilson to move. Nothing happened. Then came the *Sussex* crisis and the realization that Wilson had almost played out his hand with submarine warfare, that the next dispute likely would end in intervention unless the president could do something beforehand to stop the war. To House's urging that he set the plan in motion, Grey— for reasons mentioned—could only procrastinate and try tactfully to say the time had not yet come. Slowly and bitterly House and Wilson came to understand that it all had been a futile effort. Britain and France, it now seemed, had not only deceived House but were as warlike and anxious to continue the conflict as their adversaries.

Frustrated in this avenue, Wilson felt compelled to find another way to bring the belligerent states to their senses. On May 27, 1916, he delivered to a nonpartisan organization, the League to Enforce Peace, what turned out to be an address of considerable significance. He explained to his listeners that while the war was a result of deep and distant forces, none of which concerned the United States, the American people were "participants . . . in the life of the world." The United States was willing, once the war had ended, to join an association of nations to promote peace and democratic principles. Wilson suggested as well that he held himself ready to initiate a movement for peace.[12] As a statement on future American foreign policy the speech was significant. Wilson had pledged the United States, as much as he had the authority to do so, to membership in a league of nations. As a means of touching off a movement to bring the war to an end, the speech was a failure. "Object of speech," Spring-Rice cabled his government, "is plainly to gain German sympathy during elections and to detach Pacifists from Republican Party." [13] Neither exactly correct nor fully incorrect, the statement indicated the unresponsive attitude belligerent governments showed the efforts toward mediation.

Meanwhile forces eroding Anglo-American relations continued a steady course. In the spring and summer the so-called Easter Rebellion in Ireland caused a series of shocks in American opinion. On April 24, 1916, a group of Irish nationalists, with German aid and encouragement, rose in insurrection in Dublin. British troops quelled the uprising after a week of fighting, and there followed the execution of several leaders after what seemed unduly secretive and hasty trials. In making news of the trials public, the government at the same time announced that the defendants had been put to death. If the British felt the action justified, many Americans thought it ruthless and inhumane for a nation said to be fighting a war for humanity. Irish-Americans were almost beside themselves with anger. Emotion was so intense as to move the Senate to pass a resolution asking clemency for the notable Irish leader Sir Roger Casement. The British government sent Casement to the gallows.

Then in late July came Britain's announcement of a blacklist of American firms suspected of dealing with enemies of

12. Ray Stannard Baker and William E. Dodd, eds., *The Public Papers of Woodrow Wilson* (6 vols., New York, 1925–27), IV, 184–88.
13. Ambassador Spring-Rice to the foreign secretary, May 29, 1916, Foreign Office Papers, 371/2794.

the Allies. Those eighty-seven companies on the list faced financial ruin. No longer able to deal with British subjects, they discovered as well that other American firms kept their distance for fear of being placed on the list. Not as broad as other Allied wartime policies, and from no point of view a violation of neutral rights, this act probably was the greatest mistake of British diplomacy during the period of American neutrality. Coming at a time of diplomatic turmoil, when Americans were grumbling about the blockade, interception of mail, and suppression of the Irish rebellion, the blacklist seemed to indicate that the British were at best indifferent to American opinion and at worst deliberately hostile. Editorials in the United States were almost unanimous in their condemnation of the policy, an attitude in which President Wilson concurred. "This black list business is the last straw," he wrote House. "I am seriously considering asking Congress to authorize me to prohibit loans and restrict exportations to the Allies. . . . Polk and I are compounding a very sharp note. I may feel obligated to make it as sharp and final as the one to Germany on the submarines. . . . Can we any longer endure their intolerable course?" [14]

For a few weeks, it seemed Wilson had decided to turn against the British. He sent the note threatened in the letter to House, though it scarcely carried the tone of messages to Germany on submarine warfare. He called to the United States Ambassador Page, that Anglophile par excellence, who Wilson correctly suspected was not giving in London an energetic defense of American neutral rights. Page came home, as House put it, to get a bath of American opinion. Once in the United States, the ambassador, anxious to plead Britain's case, found himself treated as if he had the plague. Wilson and House avoided him, and Lansing tried to move him off the subject. "The Secretary betrayed not the slightest curiosity about our relations with Great Britain," wrote the exasperated envoy. "Oh God! What a crime and what a shame to have this

14. July 23, 1916, House Papers. Frank L. Polk, counselor of the State Department, was acting secretary during the brief absence of Lansing.

manikin in that place now." [15] Of much greater importance than the summoning of Page was the administration's apparent willingness to move in the direction of retaliation. Early in September, Congress with administration support passed a series of measures giving the president broad authority to apply economic sanctions against nations guilty of the sort of things Britain was doing.

It is difficult to say whether these acts represented steps toward a new direction in American foreign policy. Until put into effect, they were no more than threats, designed to influence American opinion and British policy. There was considerable difference between threat and application. Several American officials began to have second thoughts about the course on which the United States seemed embarked, fearing the president might impose a policy damaging to the Allies and contrary to the interests of the United States. House experienced uneasy feelings, and Lansing in September inserted in his diary a private memorandum entitled "The President's attitude toward Great Britain and Its Dangers." "I am almost unhappy over the situation," wrote the secretary of state. "On no account must we range ourselves even indirectly on the side of Germany, no matter how great the provocation may be." [16] Lansing did more. He explained, upon meeting the British ambassador on September 23, that while American irritation was genuine and intense, the president would use the retaliatory legislation only as a last resort. The acts, he said, were a result of the election and the president's need to appease public opinion.

This information was pleasant news in London, where British officials had been watching rising American discontent with surprise, fear, and irritation. Grey already had sent Spring-Rice a sharp protest, and on one occasion Lord Cecil unofficially had remarked that if the situation worsened Britain would break relations. All British officials knew, however, that it was meaningless to raise threats or consider any policy until they understood the options at their disposal. They began

15. Memorandum, Aug. 30, 1916, Page Papers.
16. Sept. 1916, The Papers of Robert Lansing, Library of Congress.

a thorough study to discover the extent to which Britain was dependent on American supplies and funds. It meanwhile was reassuring to learn that there was no immediate threat. Officials took Spring-Rice's message to confirm what they long had accepted as true: that American foreign policy was little more than a reflection of the domestic political climate, particularly in an election year.

The behavior most difficult to assess in the diplomatic tension of the fall of 1916 is that of the president. While Wilson did not know about Lansing's intimations to Spring-Rice (and had he known certainly would have disapproved), there was at least a measure of truth in what the secretary of state had said. Public opinion demanded that Uncle Sam stiffen his back, wave the colors, and twist the Lion's tail, and the president knew the political cost of not doing so. There nonetheless was more involved than politics; Wilson was weary of Britain's persistent, arrogant, and now it seemed costly handling of American rights, and he gave several persons reason for believing that the time might come when he would have to put the retaliatory legislation into effect. That he in fact would have done so, in face of the momentous effect retaliation would have had on the United States and the Allies, is difficult to believe. In any event the election provided a convenient reason for delaying a decision, and the president wisely concluded he should not institute policy he could not—if defeated —continue. He would see what happened in November and then decide what to do with the British.

The presidential election of 1916 was one of the closest and hardest fought in American history. It pitted Wilson against the Republican candidate, Charles Evans Hughes, a man of no mean intellect and political respectability—former progressive governor of New York who at the time of his nomination was a justice of the Supreme Court. No matter how great the problems of foreign relations, domestic issues in American elections are never far away, and Wilson in his campaign had to devote attention to national political and economic affairs. Fortunately he had understood this fact, and weeks before the election had championed important social and economic legislation. The president thus offered himself as the progressive candidate while portraying Hughes, despite a liberal background, as the defender of conservatism.

The election showed the close relation between domestic politics and foreign policy. Hughes sought—as did Wilson—to offer those policies which would win election. He had to measure statements on foreign policy as much in terms of popular appeal as in terms of strength as workable diplomacy—perhaps more. He wished to draw support from groups dissatisfied with Wilson's foreign policy, including Irish- and German-Americans, and still not woo these groups so energetically as to alienate persons who wished a firm German policy. He also had to live with, if not endorse, the pro-Ally bias of such nationalist Republican leaders as Theodore Roosevelt and Henry Cabot Lodge. Roosevelt, with his appeals for a militant foreign policy, was invariably troublesome. His most striking display came near the end of the campaign in a speech in New York. "There should be shadows now at Shadow Lawn [in New Jersey, where Wilson was staying]," said the former president, his voice trembling with emotion, "the shadows of the men, women and children who have risen from the ooze of the ocean bottom and from graves in foreign lands; the shadows of the helpless whom Mr. Wilson did not dare protect lest he might have to face danger; the shadows of babies gasping pitifully as they sank under the waves; the shadows of women outraged and slain by bandits. . . . Those are the shadows proper for Shadow Lawn; the shadows of deeds that were never done; the shadows of lofty words that were followed by no action; the shadows of the tortured dead." [17]

Trying to please everyone, Hughes appeared vacillating and inconsistent. His platform called for a "straight and honest" neutrality. At one time he said he would have severed relations after the sinking of the *Lusitania;* another time he favored a firm stand against nations which interfered with American trade. The wavering suggested, in the first place, the magnitude of problems facing the United States, and in the second place, that Wilson probably was doing as well as any-

17. Cited in Harbaugh, *Power and Responsibility,* 493–94.

one could.

Wilson's campaign was clever and much more effective. A man of personal magnetism, at least when viewed from a distance, a superb manager of words, the president at times of inspiration could move crowds to great enthusiasm. Forced to stand on his record in foreign policy, he pointed with pride to his upholding of peace and honor. He twice had forced the mighty Germans to back down and now, it seemed, was in process of putting the British in their place. It was logical and perhaps inevitable to advance one step further and say that Wilson's re-election would mean a continuance of these policies, his defeat a change. Virtually every Democrat, including the president, campaigned on the implication, if they did not say it directly, that Hughes's election would mean intervention in the European conflict. "He kept us out of war" became a ringing Democratic battle cry all over the United States.

The president nonetheless had a close call. He won with some 9.1 million votes to 8.5 million for Hughes. The vote in the Electoral College was equally close—277 to 254. While the balloting took place November 7, it was impossible to decide the winner until November 10. Hughes did not send a message of concession and congratulation until fifteen days after the election. By any standard it was a narrow escape. Wilson's victory is much more impressive when one considers the following facts: He received nearly three million more votes than he had polled in 1912. The victory came at a time when the Republican Party was the majority party, when a Republican ordinarily could expect to win the presidency. Until Wilson's victory in 1912—which, because of a split in the Republican Party, was a fluke—the Democrats had not won the presidency for twenty years. After Wilson's victory in 1916 they would not win again for sixteen more. The people had granted Wilson great honor and reward by returning him to the White House. Or had they? He faced another full term of guiding affairs of state in one of the most troublesome periods of American history, a time when relations with the Allies were at lowest ebb, when the lull in relations with Germany might end at any moment.

5

Movements toward
Peace and War

~~~~~~

IF THE ELECTION of 1916 made anything clear to Wilson
it was that the American people wanted to avoid involvement
in the World War. Everywhere he had gone during the campaign, Americans had responded with enthusiasm to that issue. The most impressive Democratic slogans and campaign
songs in some way had made mention of Wilson's efforts to
keep the nation at peace. Even former Secretary Bryan, the
symbol of noninvolvement in the United States, had done
yeoman duty for his party and president in an effort to persuade followers of Wilson's peaceful intentions. This outpouring of sentiment was fully pleasing to Wilson, for it confirmed
a belief that his policies heretofore had been correct. It vin-
dicated earlier decisions to chart his own course, often in the
face of different advice from House, Lansing—sometimes, it
seemed, almost everyone about him. For good reason some of
Wilson's deepest thoughts during the campaign and after the
election were devoted to finding a way to keep the United
States out of war. Inevitably he turned again to the idea of
mediation.

It would have been an act of infinite mercy if someone had
been able to lead the warring powers to peace in 1916, for over
two years of conflict had brought them nothing more than
enormous loss of life. The war had been a stalemate most of
the time. After the Allies had stopped the German advance at

the Marne in 1914, there developed a long, irregular Western front stretching from the North Sea to the Alps. The opposing armies constructed a massive battlefield of machine-gun nests, artillery emplacements, and an incredibly complex system of trenches. There were forward trenches, support trenches, communication trenches, supply trenches, trenches zig-zagged and criss-crossed, all of them miserable places in which to spend the war. If the men survived an infantry attack, they still had to endure the mud and cave-ins, the stench of dead horses and men, such diseases as trench foot and dysentery, and the possibility of being blown apart or buried alive by an artillery shell. Some of the holes were so deep that the men in them lived like rodents. They also lived with rodents, for rats and roaches were everywhere, and many a weary soldier, trying to sleep, awakened to find a fat rat—there was plentiful food for these indiscriminating scavengers—nibbling on his ear.

It was the costliest and most depressing sort of combat, without meaning, accomplishment, or sign of end. A few months in the trenches produced a hopelessness of the sort described in Erich M. Remarque's classic *All Quiet on the Western Front,* or in the early novels of Ernest Hemingway. One army would besiege the other with artillery, and the infantry would climb out of the trenches to capture however many feet of ground the enemy could be forced to yield. The enemy—whichever army—did not yield much, and by the beginning of 1916 the Western front was in nearly the same place it had been at the start of the conflict. The year 1916 had been a time of gigantic offensives, designed as much to exhaust the opposition as to capture territory. The battles had accomplished the former object in grand fashion, no less on the advancing army than on the defenders. The British Somme offensive lasted between June and November, in the course of which Britain suffered four hundred thousand casualties, sixty thousand falling in a single day. The gain of ground was negligible. Simultaneous with this massacre came the German assault at Verdun. By the time that seven-month battle had ended, in September 1916, Germany and France together had accumulated nearly a million casualties, and Verdun still was in French hands. It was much the same story in the East. While Russia had mounted impressive offensives in summer 1916, a series of battles which cost the Central Powers six hundred thousand men, the impact on Russia itself was devastating; the armies of the tsar were bled white, losing a million men and in the process so demoralized and physically weakened as to pave the way for a collapse of the military effort and the tsarist regime. The European giants seemingly were going nowhere, unless to their destruction.

They nonetheless would not hear of peace on terms short of their own. The stalemate in the war, an imposing argument for a tolerable peace, became a rationale for continuance of the conflict. Each belligerent had come to measure its part in the war in terms of investment, and the longer the war lasted, the higher the cost and the less satisfactory an indecisive settlement. Each month of battle added to the difficulty of ending the stalemate. It also was possible for the belligerents to reason that inasmuch as they had not lost the war, it might be possible to win, and so each nation continued the quest for the right offensive or the right mysterious new weapon that might do the job.

The German government was willing to consider negotiation as long as it could write the terms of peace. Bethmann had sent messages to Washington urging the president to act, hinting that in absence of a presidential peace initiative Germany might find it necessary to resume submarine warfare. Even before the presidential election, there was an indication that something was astir in the Second Reich, that a revision of policy might already have taken place. Submarines had stepped up activity in accord with rules of cruiser warfare, and on October 28, 1916, there occurred what could have become a crisis when a U-boat struck without warning the armed British merchantman *Marina,* taking to their death six Americans who served with the ship's crew. Peace feelers from

Berlin were an outgrowth of the desperate position in which Bethmann continued to find himself. The admiralty placed unrelenting pressure in efforts to find ways—preferably an unrestricted campaign—to make more effective use of the submarine fleet. The navy argued with great forcefulness that if the kaiser would unshackle the U-boat commanders they would strangle Britain within a few months and create conditions favorable to victory. Bethmann of course questioned the accuracy of this ambitious prognostication; he knew as well that there was no way, short of allowing the navy to try, to prove it wrong. The longer he held off the admirals, the more tempting their argument, and the chancellor realized that if the war continued in a stalemate, the kaiser would succumb in time to the urgings of his military chieftains. How much better it would be if beforehand he could arrange a peace favorable to Germany.

Bethmann had no faith in Wilson's proposing an acceptable settlement; he did not even want the president to offer terms. He had in mind simply an announcement of a conference and pressure from the United States to have the Allies attend. Once negotiation had begun, he wanted Wilson to stand aside and allow the belligerents to strike terms of peace. In that case Germany could speak from strength, for even though the war by 1916 had produced no winner, the Germans much of the time had controlled territory ordinarily not theirs. The Western front left much of Belgium and parts of France in German hands, and by the autumn of 1916 German armies had begun an advance into Russian Poland. Any consideration of peace, which would have to take these conditions into account, could not be unfavorable to Germany. Thus the chancellor saw Wilson's intervention as at best a device to help him secure a limited German victory; at worst it could head off a course of events that might lead to defeat.

From all appearances the Allies were as hostile to negotiation as they ever had been. This sentiment had seemed unmistakably clear in a public statement by David Lloyd George,

British minister for war, a bold, forceful Welshman who did not have, at the time, and never would obtain a reputation for tact. Speaking to an American reporter on September 28 (during the presidential campaign), Lloyd George expressed fear that Wilson might "butt in" and attempt to stop the war. Britain would tolerate no outside interference, he said. "Peace now or at any time before the final and complete elimination of this [German] menace is unthinkable. . . . The fight must be to the finish—to a knockout." [1] In some measure the Allied attitude stemmed from the realistic conclusion that no acceptable peace could grow out of battlefield conditions at that time. Despite an increasing weariness, the British and French people were unwilling to end the war with nothing to show for their efforts. No government wished to risk asking as much of them. Then too, Britain and France refused to relinquish hope that by tightening the blockade and stepping up military activity on the Continent they could put the enemy on the run.

The Allies persisted in this rigid posture despite an awareness of their economic vulnerability. Stunned by the retaliatory legislation passed by Congress in September 1916, the British government had begun a study to determine the degree to which the war effort depended upon American assistance. The findings, in the government's hands by early October, were no less shocking than overwhelming. Britain could not continue the war without the United States. Deprived of American assistance in funds and supplies, Britain and likely also the other Allies would either lose the war or have to accept a highly unfavorable peace. As one official summarized the situation: "In munitions . . . all previous estimates of our being able to fill our own needs by a certain time have been entirely destroyed. . . . In steel . . . we have been obliged to buy up the whole of the United States' steel output; in foodstuffs and especially in wheat . . . in all industrial raw materials and above all in cotton and lubricants American supplies are

1. *New York Times,* Sept. 29, 1916.

so necessary to us that reprisals, while they would produce tremendous distress in America, would also practically stop the war." An equally distressing report from the British Treasury concluded that without American loans it would be futile to continue.[2] All this information suggests, of course, what great power rested in the hands of President Wilson and the American government, that Wilson was in a position to command the Allies to do virtually as he wished.

But it is necessary to qualify this broad generalization. In the first place, Wilson was not fully aware of the power at his disposal; if he realized that the Allies were much in need of American assistance, he did not know of their desperate plight as revealed in the British government's study. Second, a drastic change in policy, such as an embargo or prohibition of loans, not only would have wrecked the British war effort but would have thrown the American economy into severe disarray, for if the United States had become a vital part of the Allies' economic structure, the reverse also was true. America's economic weapons probably were too large to use. British officials understood this fact, and for this reason the deliberations of October 1916 drove them neither to fits of despair nor to a hasty sweetening of relations with the United States. In fact the British planned no immediate change other than small efforts to polish their image in America and a more energetic campaign to woo these groups and individuals in a position to loan money to the Allies. Finally, had Wilson realized his power to dictate to the Allies, it is doubtful he would have used it. The president's estimate of the Allies indeed had soured by 1916, and he was willing to hold Britain and France partly responsible for the outbreak and prolongation of the conflict. He had told Page in September that the war was a

2. "Minutes of the Interdepartmental Committee on the Dependence of the British Empire on the United States," Oct. 4, 1916, Foreign Office Papers, 371/2795; "The Financial Dependence of the United Kingdom on the United States of America," Oct. 10, 1916, "Printed for the use of the War Committee of the Cabinet, November 1916," *ibid.*, 371/2796.

result of "England's having the earth and of Germany want-
ing it." [3] He nonetheless was anything but pro-German and
would have recoiled at the thought of any American action
which might impose defeat upon Britain and France. All the
blustering during the summer of 1916 about the intolerable
British course and need for decisive action came to nothing.
What Wilson needed was power to command both groups of
belligerents. Time would show that he had that power, but
the Germans did not know it (Bethmann perhaps to the contrary), and Wilson could not use it without going to war.

Wilson could think of only one thing: to bring the war to
an end. His inclination toward a "one-track mind," his unwillingness to pursue a course contrary to advice from virtually
all quarters, was never more evident than in the campaign for
mediation in the fall of 1916. Wilson pressed the mediation
movement because, above all reasons, he desperately wanted
peace to begin. The British virtually had sent a refusal in advance. The German government, while professing an interest
in negotiation, had been silent about terms of peace and vague
about the president's role. Lansing, House, and Counselor
Polk tried tactfully to move Wilson off his course. Lansing in
fact had wanted to press the *Marina* case, if necessary to a
break in relations. The consensus among the three major advisers was that Wilson, if he continued, might find himself
maneuvered into an alignment with the Germans. Hence pro-
Allied sentiment within the administration, driven to hiding
now and then by the behavior of the Allies themselves, showed
itself ever willing to resist anything potentially beneficial to the
Germans.

House had some idea of the difficulty in changing Wilson's
mind, and in discussion with the president in November he
did not try very hard. Wilson explained that unless there were
some sharp change in the war, submarine warfare would force
the United States to intervention. Before allowing that catastrophe he felt he must make one last effort at mediation, even

3. Page Diary; Hendrick, *Page,* II, 186.

though it might arouse resentment in Britain and France. He meanwhile was willing to set aside other diplomatic disputes. He would not press the case of the *Marina,* he said, because that attack had involved a merchantman, and the agreement with Germany pertained only to passenger ships—a statement which, of course, was false. Moreover, Wilson told his friend, "I do not believe the American people would wish to go to war no matter how many Americans were lost at sea." [4] House made some feeble effort to challenge these statements and let the matter drop.

Meeting a few days later, the two men turned to find the best procedure. Wilson wondered if it might be a good idea for House to return to London. House said he would go if the president thought it best; privately he wrote that he would rather be in hell. They eventually dismissed the idea of another European mission on the grounds that time was too short. House again warned that the United States might "drift into a sympathetic alliance" with Germany and that the Allies under provocation might declare war. He also warned of possible trouble with Walter Page, who probably would go into fits at any new mention of mediation. Wilson dismissed House's arguments as either unlikely or unimportant. He did not care about Page. "No man," he said, "must stand in the way." [5]

In late November Wilson set about the task of preparing a peace note for the belligerent powers. A delicate chore, it became more difficult when he contracted a serious cold. He also had to work largely alone. House and Lansing were available for advice, but since both preferred that the president send no message, their help was not the sort that Wilson wanted. Wilson had been at work several days when the German government announced its peace proposal. It was a simple message which called for a conference of belligerents and made no mention of American participation—the sort of offer that Britain and France almost certainly would reject. Wilson was not

4. House Diary, Nov. 2, 1916.
5. *Ibid.,* Nov. 14, 1916.

pleased to learn of the German note, for he thought it only complicated his task. If he acted immediately he stood the risk of appearing to act in conjunction with the Central Powers. If he did not act, the Allies might reject the German proposal and close off all opportunity for a negotiated peace. Deciding the latter risk was greater, the president hurriedly put finishing touches to his peace message. In final form the dispatch was considerably less ambitious than the proposal he had wanted to send. He had thought of urging, of almost demanding, a peace conference and asserting the right of the United States to participate, but while he still hoped these developments might materialize, he did not make them part of the peace message.

The president had Lansing send the proposal on December 18, only two days after the Allies had received the German note. The message asserted independence of the recent German proposal, stating that while no belligerent had been clear as to war aims, all powers seemed to be fighting for the same general goals. It seemed reasonable to believe that the path to a peace settlement should begin with all belligerents stating their war aims. Wilson counted on the nations being so anxious to conceal their greed that they would find themselves without reason to reject negotiation. He did not insist upon American participation, but he did say that the United States was ready, "even eager," to help achieve reasonable objectives.[6]

However proper the war-aims proposal seemed to Wilson, it impressed his close advisers as laden with danger for relations with the Allies. Thinking the president wrong and—for the moment, at least—untrustworthy, they moved to head off what they feared would become a series of catastrophic events. Handing the message to Lord Cecil, Page made no effort to promote the president's wishes; indeed, he virtually apologized for the contents of the note. Colonel House was concerned that the Allies would find Wilson's reference to identical war

6. The secretary of state to Ambassadors and Ministers in Belligerent Countries, Dec. 18, 1916, *For. Rels., 1916, Supp.,* 97–99.

aims (an implication that they fought for no higher purposes than the Germans) disgusting and perhaps provocative. He feared that if Germany accepted Wilson's offer to negotiate, and the Allies refused, the United States almost by default would find itself aligned with the Germans. House then sought to assure an English friend in the United States—who cabled the message to the Foreign Office—that the American attitude had not changed from what it had been in February 1916, the time of House's last mission to Europe. However imprecise that statement, it left the impression that the United States still wanted a settlement that was favorable to the Allies. It was a false portrayal of the wishes of the president, who at that time would have been pleased to reach terms favorable to neither side. Even more disloyal action came from the secretary of state. Evidently concluding that the message was insulting to the Allies, a seeming adjunct to the German proposal, and a threat to relations with Britain and France, Lansing moved to soften if not stifle Wilson's preliminary peace effort. He issued without the president's authorization a public statement on December 21 that Wilson's message should not be construed as a peace note; on the contrary, the president had acted because the United States was on the verge of war. Lansing seemed to say that Wilson wanted to use belligerents' war aims as a guide to determine which side to join. He privately expressed similar thoughts to the British and French ambassadors, albeit in such fashion as to reaffirm America's pro-Ally inclination.

To say that these events aroused and confused Allied officials would be an understatement. The British government had undergone a change before the peace note arrived. Leaving office were Prime Minister Herbert Asquith, and a cabinet grown unpopular for its timid prosecution of the war. Into power came a coalition cabinet headed by Lloyd George, the aggressive "Welsh witch," identified in British opinion as a devotee of the "knock-out" blow. Edward Grey went out with the change, and while he received the honor of an elevation to

the House of Lords, he in fact was gently pushed into retire-
ment. Grey's replacement in the Foreign Office was Arthur
Balfour, a kindly-looking old gentleman who fell ill shortly
after taking office and temporarily turned his duties over to
Lord Cecil, Britain's watchdog of the blockade. The Lloyd
George Cabinet symbolized sentiment for stiffening foreign
policy and carrying the war to a bitter end; it was not a regime
inclined toward mediation. Wilson, who seemed oblivious to
that feeling, had insisted upon treading where he had been un-
invited. Worse, he had acted with an air of cold detachment:
he had said that both sides were fighting for similar objectives,
an attitude which suggested that he was blind to, or afraid to
acknowledge, the Allied crusade against German militarism.
The war-aims proposal inspired expressions of dismay in Britain and France. On hearing of the message, King George of
England reportedly broke down and wept. The efforts of House
and Lansing to soften the blow had only confused matters,
and then came a second public statement by the secretary of
state (Wilson had ordered him to issue the message) that
amounted to a retraction of Lansing's first statement on the
war-aims proposal. Piecing bits of information together, British and French officials concluded that the American president
probably was trying to promote peace negotiation but, more
important, did not intend to compel the Allies to submit, as
they knew he had the power to do. Consequently they felt it
safe to proceed as planned. After long deliberation, waiting
for the Germans to reply first, the Allies announced a list of
aims which demanded considerable German concession.
There was no hope the Germans would accept. The Allies were
trying to tell Wilson, without antagonizing him, that they had
little faith in a negotiated peace.

The Germans had been no more encouraging than the
Allies. Bethmann did not wish to reveal to Wilson and the
world the terms on which he would settle, and the chancellor
was anxious to avoid encouraging Wilson's intervention. Even
had Bethmann been willing to comply with the American re-

quest, the German military by that time could exercise a veto on major acts of government. Germany's reply of December 26, 1916, offered to state war aims only at a council of belligerents in which, presumably, the president would take no part.

However much they tried, the belligerents could not persuade the president to give up. He insisted upon continuing the campaign, stubbornly maintaining that the answers were not as final as they might appear. House seemed to agree. Convinced by the Allied reply that relations with Britain and France were not in jeopardy, the Colonel now was willing to aid and encourage the president. Wilson also received encouragement from the German ambassador. Not well informed on happenings within his own government, Bernstorff urged Wilson to keep the peace movement alive as the only means of preventing a resumption of submarine warfare and a conflict with the United States. These were the factors behind Wilson's address to the Senate on January 22, 1917, the most memorable aspect of which was the president's plea for a "peace without victory." Here he hoped to continue and perhaps strengthen the momentum of the peace campaign, muster support by the American antiwar populace, and inspire the war-weary people in belligerent countries to move their governments to negotiation. He encouraged the combatants to reach terms without his help, if that was the way they must have it. The speech was notable in its pledge of American cooperation in maintaining a reasonable peace. Though a premature utterance which showed no awareness of potential congressional opposition to membership in a league of nations, the pledge reflected Wilson's conviction that the United States thereafter would have to accept full and permanent participation in world politics. The speech was prophetic in its description of the type of treaty Wilson felt would succeed. There would be no value, he said, in reaching a one-sided settlement, for the loser would feel a compulsion to gain back what it had lost. The only treaty that could last, the only settlement the United States could help uphold, would be a peace among equals based on the highest principles of justice and humanity.

The "peace without victory" speech at the time aroused flattering statements from many quarters; it since has been judged one of Wilson's most memorable utterances.[7] The fact remains that for its primary purpose it was a superfluous message, incapable of loosening the deadlock on the battle-field. Perhaps nothing Wilson could have done at that stage of the war would have led the nations to a peace settlement. It was nonetheless true that he made little effort to apply leverage; he did not brandish the weapons in his arsenal, partly because he did not know how large they were. He relied on powers of persuasion and on broadcasting willingness to act as an impartial mediator. It was not enough for nations with so much at stake. They did not want a just peace unless a just peace was defined as a settlement that left the enemy defeated.

The peace campaign contributed much to Wilson's image in the European countries as a self-righteous phrasemaker, an impression that unfortunately would carry over to the peace negotiations in Paris in 1919. The request for war aims and peace without victory carried an implication that all belligerents were greedy, short-sighted, and that only Wilson could lift the European giants out of their wrongful ways. In truth, the Allies did not mind Wilson's attacking evil in the world as long as they could define what was evil. This time the president's moralizing went in the wrong direction. The attitude toward Wilson reflected an important development in world affairs: the decline of Europe's ability to manage world affairs and the growing influence of the United States. When the

7. Of course, this attitude was not universal. Officials in Britain and France viewed "peace without victory" in much the same way as they had regarded the quest for war aims—that Wilson did not understand the need to destroy German militarism. Ambassador Page recalled that " 'peace without victory' brought us to the very depths of European disfavor." Memorandum, Page Papers.

Allies grumbled about the president's meddling, they were provoked no more by his saintly posture than by the realization that he could force them to yield if he chose. The debate over American power had created havoc within the German government. It might have evoked a conclusion similar to the one Britain had reached—that the United States could determine which side would win—but for the influence of military officials, whose magnified estimate of German armed strength finally prevailed in making policy. As a result, the peace campaign had failed even before it was under way; before Wilson had addressed the Senate on January 22, 1917, the German government had made a decision with respect to submarine policy which virtually ended all hope of a mediated settlement.

That tragic change in 1917 was attributable to no single event, but to a progression of forces at work since 1915. The Germany navy by 1917 had enlarged the undersea fleet and improved the quality of submarines. Naval officials had continued to make grandiose claims of what the U-boats could accomplish, and by the autumn of 1916 virtually all the admirals agreed that submarine warfare would allow Germany to win the war. That the Germans had not acted sooner was due largely to the foresight and political expertise of the chancellor. Bethmann had held off the navy for the greater part of two years, maneuvered the resignation of Tirpitz, and in August 1916 helped bring about the removal of Falkenhayn from command of the army. Yet it was clear that the chancellor almost had played out his hand. Though it had followed his lead, Germany had not won the war. Unlike the naval officials, he could offer no hope of spectacular success; the best the Germans could expect from his policies was more of the same tedious struggle. He had come under attack in the Reichstag, and rumors were circulating that the chancellor would be the next person to leave office.

Bethmann realized that he also was losing control over the kaiser. If Wilhelm had never been a perceptive ruler, he occasionally had demonstrated signs of strength and leadership.

Now, with the war entering a dreary third year, he became increasingly detached and concerned with trivial matters. One can follow the process of deterioration in the diary of Admiral Georg von Müller, naval adviser to the crown, a man in almost daily contact with the kaiser. In the late summer of 1916 Müller made the following notations:

> *August 4:* Conversation in the dining car. His majesty intends to reform society in Berlin after the war. The members of the aristocracy are to build palaces for themselves once more. He will forbid parties being given in hotels. He then proceeded to read us an article on the need for encouraging motor-racing in Berlin. And all this in such gloomy, difficult times.

> *August 7:* Great indignation with the Kaiser who spends hours supervising the building of a fountain at Homburg, for which a war contractor has raised the money. He went for an excursion to Saalburg and Friedrichshof this afternoon and refused to read a report from Hindenburg on the situation on the Eastern Front because "he had no time."

> *September 15:* This afternoon His Majesty bagged his second and third stag, and appeared this evening wearing his *Pour le Merite,* two Iron Crosses and the Hunter's Jubilee Badge.

> *September 16:* Hindenburg consulted the Crown Prince of Bavaria as to how we can bring some relief to the Somme. Does he want more infantry? No. More artillery? No, but more ammunition. The Kaiser continues to shoot stag.[8]

Wilhelm spent almost all his time on holiday or at military headquarters, where he received frequent visits from the kaiserin. He became a captive of the military men about him, who related what news they wanted him to hear. He rarely saw Bethmann (who stayed in Berlin), was apparently content to approve with little thought the decisions of the military high command.

Seeing his power dwindle, Bethmann had tried to act be-

8. Goerlitz, *The Kaiser and His Court,* 189, 190, 203, 204.

fore he became completely powerless and the military ran Germany to catastrophe. He had prompted Wilson to seek peace negotiations, and then sponsored his own proposal. Had he been in complete command, he might have settled for peace without victory or even invited Wilson to mediate. Bethmann did not have that power in December 1916, and while he was the government's spokesman on all matters concerning peace, his position was conditioned by what the high command would accept. The generals would hear of no negotiation that might end unfavorable to Germany.

When Falkenhayn had lost his post in August 1916, the kaiser had no difficulty finding a successor. The logical choice was Field Marshal Paul von Hindenburg, hero of Tannenberg and other battles on the eastern front, the most popular military man in Germany. To get Hindenburg one also had to take his comrade-in-arms, General Erich Ludendorff, who had contributed mightily to the field marshal's major victories. The two officers thereupon established dual leadership of the high command, Hindenburg providing glamour and prestige, Ludendorff the skill and dynamic energy. Bethmann had welcomed the transfer of command, hoping Hindenburg would be more agreeable than Falkenhayn had become. In one way he had not been disappointed, because the new generals did not insist upon an immediate resumption of submarine warfare. But in one crucial sense he had, for Hindenburg and Ludendorff were scheming and overbearing, willing to intervene in political matters far beyond what Falkenhayn ever had attempted. The generals were so forceful and the kaiser so weak that by the beginning of 1917 Germany was a monarchy only in name. The nation in fact had become a virtual military dictatorship. The high command still followed the ritual of acting through the crown, but Wilhelm found no alternative to approving the proposals of his military chieftains.

By December Ludendorff and Hindenburg had decided the time had come for unrestricted submarine warfare, and by December, with the failure of his peace overture, Bethmann realized that the struggle was almost lost. The chancellor nonetheless fought a strenuous last battle. He argued privately with Ludendorff and Hindenburg, and then appeared at an imperial conference on January 9, 1917, at the kaiser's residence at Pless. It was a familiar story, much the same as he had been presenting since 1915: Germany could not endure the intervention of the United States, an event certain to take place if Germany resumed unrestricted submarine warfare. Though Bethmann's economic adviser recited statistics about American resources, the British merchant marine, and the results one might expect from submarines, it was a futile effort. Naval spokesmen promised that Bethmann's calculations were wrong, that the submarines could force Britain to its knees within six months, before American participation could have a noticeable effect. All military officials agreed—at least they declined to disagree—with this conclusion, and when Hindenburg and Ludendorff added their approval, the kaiser gave the order to resume unrestricted submarine warfare.

In retrospect it is not difficult to see that the naval spokesmen's premise was false and the kaiser's decision unwise, but one must say that the Germans had no easy choice. The prospect of continuing the war in its present costly, indecisive state was not pleasant. The navy had increased the fleet by more than a hundred submarines, many of them vastly improved over the slow, flimsy vessels that had inaugurated submarine warfare in 1915. Even so, the decision is a classic example of a nation placing military consideration above all other concerns. While some diplomatic maneuvering continued during the rest of January, particularly after Wilson offered his "peace without victory" speech, it did not change the decision of January 9, 1917. Bernstorff in Washington sadly handed the submarine message to Lansing on January 31.

The German proclamation placed before Wilson one of the most difficult decisions of his presidency. In this troubled time he again turned to House for comfort and advice, and from House's diary we learn the president's mood: "The President was sad and depressed, and I did not succeed at any time during the day in lifting him into a better frame of mind. He was deeply disappointed in the sudden and unwarranted action of the German Government. . . . The President said he felt as if the world had suddenly reversed itself; that after going from east to west, it had begun to go from west to east, and that he could not get his balance. . . . The President was insistent that he would not allow it [the German Proclamation] to lead to war if it could possibly be avoided. He reiterated his belief that it would be a crime for this Government to involve itself in the war to such an extent as to make it impossible to save Europe afterward. He spoke of Germany as 'a madman that should be curbed.' I asked if he thought it fair to the Allies to ask them to do the curbing without doing our share. He noticeably winced at this, but still held to his determination not to become involved if it were humanly possible to do otherwise. We sat listlessly during the morning until Lansing arrived. . . . The President nervously arranged his books and walked up and down the floor. . . . We are listlessly killing time. . . ." [9]

For all his indecision, Wilson had but one reasonable course. The proclamation announced Germany's intent to sink all ships in a war zone around the British Isles. In effect it cancelled the *Arabic* pledge, *Sussex* promise, and all the earlier concessions on submarine warfare. All American ships hereafter were subject to attack, and some surely would be struck —so one could conclude from the German message. Virtually every official with whom Wilson discussed the matter said that the United States would have to break relations. Lansing was openly anxious to get into the war. Still the president looked for reasons for holding back. He argued that the United States and the world would benefit most if the war ended in a draw and not, as Lansing wished, in crushing of German military power. While there was strength in this argument (and in

9. Seymour, *The Intimate Papers of Colonel House,* II, 439, 440, 441.

retrospect it probably was correct), it could not change the fact that Germany had presented a direct challenge, compelling Wilson to honor the pledges he had made on submarine warfare or withdraw them. On February 3 he announced severance of relations with Germany.

Almost two months followed before Wilson asked Congress for a declaration of war; meanwhile the president continued a desperate search for honorable ways to avoid intervention. In some measure Wilson acted—as he had for several months —out of simple dread of war, the awesome responsibility of leading the nation into the bloody conflict. At the same time he continued to believe that only as a neutral participant could he preside over the sort of balanced settlement that had a chance of lasting. He had told the Senate on February 3 that he intended to wait for "overt acts" to prove Germany's hostile intent. What he meant by these words he did not make clear beyond expressing his intent to protect American lives and property. Events of the following weeks showed that he had retreated from some of the demands he had previously pressed on the Germans. He did not act when German torpedoes struck belligerent merchantmen, which meant that he was willing to abandon the concessions he had gained in the *Sussex* incident. He did not act when a submarine attacked a British passenger ship. The *Arabic* pledge seemed to have vanished beneath the waves. Wilson kept close watch on these events and privately pointed out that the sinkings often took place under highly dubious circumstances: several of the ships attacked were armed, perhaps for offensive purposes; some vessels almost invited attack, by attempting to escape, for example. Such argument was so strained and concerned with technical detail that it suggests the president was seeking to rationalize his inaction. While he made no public effort to describe what events would provoke him to war, some perceptive observers concluded that he would act on nothing less than a deliberate assault on an American ship. Meanwhile he probed for something to lessen his terrible problems. He inspired an effort to detach Austria-Hungary from the Central Powers and thereby hasten peace. He pondered an alternative to outright declaration of hostilities—some policy short of war, such as armed neutrality. Whether he was seeking new permanent policy to last until the end of the war, or whether he sought an expedient way—with a temporary yielding of rights —to ride out the crisis is impossible to say. Probably he himself did not know.

From all appearances most of the American people approved of Wilson's performance. The events of 1917 sharpened opinion in the United States but did not change it much. Interventionists and nationalists of course were almost beside themselves with anger. Who was this man who spoke for the United States? For what principles did he stand when faced with danger? One conclusion was certain: he fell far short of the manly American standards Roosevelt had upheld, and on which Roosevelt again was expounding. Encouraged by the breach in relations, interventionists had difficulty controlling their frustration as they detected Wilson's hesitation to advance the logical next step. From the other side pacifists, German-Americans, and all those opposed to war with Germany made their voices heard in rallies, newspapers, and whatever means of communication they could command. They worried about the rumor that Wilson planned to have guns placed on American merchantmen—if not an act of war, surely an act that would lead to war—and demanded that the president keep Americans and American ships away from the war zone. It is impossible to measure the size of these opposition groups. Of perhaps equal strength, both were forceful and sincere, both afforded the American people an opportunity to support a course different from what Wilson was following. The bulk of the population chose not to do so. They were willing to follow the president, some because they believed and trusted him, many because in this bewildering time they did not know what else to do. They hoped that Wilson could find an honorable way to avoid war.

Events thereupon made an honorable alternative ever more elusive, and easily the most dramatic new development was the episode of the Zimmermann telegram. The German foreign secretary, Arthur Zimmermann, had sent this famous message to his representative in Mexico on January 17, 1917, after Germany had decided to resume submarine warfare but before the decision had become public. In this cable he proposed a military alliance with Mexico, in the event the forthcoming submarine warfare provoked war between Germany and the United States. Germany offered the Mexican government financial assistance and support in reacquiring territory lost in the war with the United States in 1846–48. The telegram also mentioned the possibility of approaching the Japanese government. Clearly the Germans wished to exploit tension already existing in Mexican-American relations, to keep the United States embroiled in its hemisphere. Zimmermann had sent the secret dispatch via a variety of routes, including the channels of the State Department in Washington, thereby brazenly exploiting a courtesy the United States earlier had extended to facilitate discussion of the mediation proposal.[10] Britain intercepted the telegram every way the Germans sent it and, waiting for a safe time to act, gave it to Ambassador Page on February 24. All American officials reacted with understandable anger and astonishment. "Good Lord," exclaimed Wilson upon learning the contents of the telegram and Zimmermann's method of transmission.[11] The president released the message to the press on February 29, and, once convinced it was authentic (and not a British forgery), American newspapers were nearly unanimous in condemnation of the base plot. Interventionists were almost

10. The United States had allowed the Germans use of its cable facilities from Berlin, so that the Germans might avoid British-controlled cables and have faster lines of communication to the United States. Unknown to the Americans or the Germans, the British also had tapped this source.

11. Robert Lansing, *War Memoirs of Robert Lansing* (Indianapolis, 1935), 228.

blind with rage. If Wilson now did not go to war, Roosevelt remarked privately, "I shall skin him alive." [12] Sending the Zimmermann telegram appeared to most Americans a cruel and hostile deed, but the episode probably has been exaggerated as a cause of American intervention. The telegram helped condition the United States to the likelihood, perhaps the wisdom, of war with Germany. It did not provoke Wilson to ask for a declaration of hostilities; that act did not come until a month afterward.

Momentum for war continued to build. Wilson on February 26 asked Congress for permission to arm American merchant ships. Since January 31 shippers had been understandably hesitant to venture unprotected into the war zones, and a costly slowdown in ocean traffic had resulted. Though Wilson knew of the Zimmermann telegram at the time of this action, the move was not necessarily a result of the provocative German document. For some time the president had considered the measure. The House of Representatives, inspired by publication of the Zimmermann telegram, passed the armed-ship bill with haste and virtual unanimity. The Senate was unable to act. Some Senators worried that the sweeping language of the bill would allow the president to fight a war without asking Congress, and a small clique led by Robert M. LaFollette of Wisconsin forced the upper house into filibuster. Near the end of its session the Senate adjourned. Angry and disappointed, Wilson followed with one of his sharpest public statements: "A little group of willful men, representing no opinion but their own, have rendered the great government of the United States helpless and contemptible." [13] While a meaningful indictment of congressional inefficiency, the statement was not a fair assessment of the government's condition at that time. The administration dusted off a statute passed in 1819, stretched the law to apply to present conditions, ordered the navy to begin arming merchant vessels and thereafter to fire

12. Cited in Harbaugh, *Power and Responsibility,* 496.
13. *New York Times,* March 5, 1917.

at any submarine within range. Wilson hoped that arming merchantmen, though surely a step toward war, might have reverse effect. If these limited measures could protect American lives and property, he might be able to avoid declaration of full-scale hostilities. It was a desperate and futile hope.

Shortly afterward news arrived in Washington that the tsarist regime had fallen and that Russia was in the hands of a provisional parliamentary government. It was impossible to say exactly what events had taken place and what they meant for the Russian political system, but ignorance in certain cases can be a blessing, allowing individuals to find in conditions what they wished. What administration officials saw in events in Russia was removal of the blight that had burdened the Allied cause since the beginning of the war. Joining the Allies heretofore had also meant fighting alongside the most backward and autocratic of all belligerent nations, including Germany. It now was possible to say that the Allies in all major respects were fighting the battle for democracy and representative government. The revolution in Russia (the first revolution; the second, Bolshevik, revolution came a few months later) was important enough for Lansing and other officials to mention it to Wilson as a means of justifying intervention.

None of the events of February and March 1917—the reopening of submarine warfare, the Zimmermann telegram, the Russian Revolution—was capable in itself of provoking war; together they did not move Wilson to take the final step. They nonetheless were important in creating an atmosphere favorable to war. They helped influence a large majority of the American people to accept and support a decision that it had preferred to avoid. They suggested differences between the Allies and Central Powers so great that people increasingly came to view intervention as not only unavoidable but perhaps also humanly beneficial. They helped induce Wilson to offer, and Americans later to accept, the interpretation that the war after all was a crusade against evil forces. Perhaps the most curious feature of these dramatic happenings was that after all had taken place, Wilson still clung to faint hope that somehow he could avert hostilities.

He was not allowed that hope for long, for he learned on March 18 that submarines had sunk three American vessels. Whatever thoughts he previously might have entertained, there now was no reason for seeing anything other than a German intent to sink all American ships within range of submarines. Even then, Wilson was hesitant. There was no emergency session with Lansing or hasty summoning of the Cabinet. The president spent much of the time by himself, and when he did talk to officials, he gave evidence of uncertainty as to the proper course. When he finally met the Cabinet two days later, on March 20, he asked each man's opinion of relations with Germany. Though all members said that the United States had no alternative to a declaration of war, Wilson closed the meeting without revealing his thoughts. Shortly afterward he called a special session of Congress for April 2 "to receive a communication concerning grave matters of national policy." Everyone then knew that Wilson had decided on war with Germany.

Few who were present in Washington on April 2 would forget the atmosphere of excitement and drama that circulated about the city. The first faint signs of spring were appearing about the White House, the lawn beginning to green, the trees bearing some evidence of an approaching greenery. The temperature was in the mid-fifties, and on some days it had climbed higher, almost in eagerness for spring. The capital was a beehive of activity, with congressmen flocking in for the special session; and the historic assemblage had attracted a huge crowd of curiosity-seekers, peace demonstrators, and an exceptionally large number of police. Tempers occasionally flared in this confused environment, and in the early afternoon Senator Lodge had rained some sprightly blows on a visitor who disagreed with the senator's idea on foreign affairs. Pennsylvania Avenue was a picture of busyness as the new automobiles, no longer a novel sight, mingled with countless carriages in a slow procession down the street toward the Houses of Congress. At 8:20 in the evening the traffic was interrupted when the president's auto, escorted by a troop of cavalry, made its way from the White House to the capital. Some ten minutes later, the president left the car and entered the chamber of the House of Representatives.

The war message of April 2 was by almost all accounts one of the most impressive speeches of Wilson's or any other presidential administration. Never had the president demonstrated a better ability to state a case with eloquence and persuasive artistry, or to move an audience to a feeling of great inspiration. He spoke to a packed chamber of congressmen, government officials, and visitors—some supporters and followers, some political opponents, some no less than bitter enemies. Wilson justified intervention by saying what he felt to be true, that the German government had forced him to it, and then he reviewed the controversy over submarine warfare and other unpardonable acts, such as spy activity, that Germany had imposed upon the United States. The president went on to say that the war was much more than a means of protecting American honor and interests. He now saw the conflict as no less than a device to treat the evils of mankind. He summoned his listeners to a crusade against oppressive institutions, such as the German government, which he felt had been the cause of human conflict and suffering. "We are glad," said the president, "now that we see the facts with no veil of false pretense about them, to fight . . . for the ultimate peace of the world and for the liberation of its peoples, the German people included: for the rights of nations great and small and the privilege of men everywhere to choose their way of life and of obedience. The world must be made safe for democracy." [14] It had been a moving oration, and when the president had finished, most of his listeners—there remained a few diehard dissenters—were ready to grasp the Hun by the collar, feeling that surely God was on their side, and if He was not, God this one time must be wrong.

14. Baker and Dodd, *Public Papers of Woodrow Wilson,* V, 6–17.

It is understandable that the president would make some such appeal. He needed an inspiring means of rallying popular support, and the American people, accustomed to politicians speaking with moral rhetoric, found nothing extraordinary in hearing that their cause was right. It nonetheless remains that Wilson thereby was placing on the war an interpretation he had not been willing to admit, in fact had vigorously denied. He offered greater reward for a successful military effort than this war, or any war, could deliver. He also was helping lay the basis for the type of peace settlement he recently had said would not last.

These are thoughts of retrospect; they occurred to few of the people Wilson was addressing in 1917. It was a time to rally to the colors and not direct picayune criticism at so noble a speech. The vote on a war resolution was much a formality, although Congress did take four days to follow rules of debate and procedure. Opponents of intervention, mostly representatives of midwestern states with large German populations, had some bitter last words. Their leader in the Senate, LaFollette of Wisconsin, spoke for more than four hours. They thrust forth various charges, many of them having to do with the "unneutral" character of American neutrality, and with the way large economic interests had influenced the course of the nation. While some of the points were true, they were essentially negative, designed to curtail policy without the need to offer an acceptable alternative. They came late and with little support. The Senate approved 82 to 6, the House 373 to 50, and the president signed the war resolution on April 6. The United States found itself fully entwined in European and world affairs. It never again would be able to extricate itself.

6

Some Final Thoughts

IN LIGHT OF the controversy which later surrounded America's entry into the First World War, and the momentous effect that war had on the future of the world, it seems appropriate here to offer some final observations about Wilsonian diplomacy and the factors responsible for intervention. Wilson asked Congress to declare war in 1917 because he felt Germany had driven him to it. He could find no way, short of an unthinkable abandonment of rights and interests, to avoid intervention. He briefly had tried armed neutrality, and as he said in the war message, that tactic had not done the job. Germany was making war on the United States, and Wilson had no reasonable alternative to a declaration of hostilities. Hence submarine warfare must bear the immediate responsibility for provoking the decision for war. It nonetheless is not enough to say that the United States went to war simply because of the submarines, or that the events of January–March 1917 alone determined the fate of the United States, for a number of factors helped bring the nation to that point where it seemed impossible to do anything else. During the period of neutrality the American government made certain decisions, avoided others, found itself pulled one way or another by national sentiment and need and by the behavior of the belligerent nations.

Any account of American intervention would go amiss without some reference to the pro-Ally nature of American neutrality. American money and supplies allowed the Allies to sustain the war effort. While Wilson did not act openly par-

tial to the Allies, he did promote American economic enterprise and declined to interfere—indeed showed no signs of
dismay—when the enterprise developed in ways that were
beneficial to Britain and France. Although Wilson did experience a considerable hardening of attitude toward the Allies
in 1916 (his major advisers did not), he could not bring himself to limit the provisioning of Britain and France; and it was
this traffic that brought on submarine warfare. Without American assistance to the Allies, Germany would have had no
reason to adopt policy injurious to the interests of the United
States.

There were several reasons why American policy functioned in a manner which favored the Allies. The first was a
matter of circumstances: Britain controlled the sea, and the
Allies were in desperate need of American products—conditions which assured that most American trade would go to
Britain and France. The second factor was an assumption by
much of the American population, most members of the administration, and the president that the political and material
well-being of the United States was associated with preservation of Britain and France as strong, independent states. Germany unintentionally confirmed the assumption with the
invasion of Belgium, use of submarines, and war tactics in general. While pro-Ally feeling was tempered by a popular desire
to stay out of the conflict and by the president's wish to remain
fair and formally neutral, it was sufficiently strong to discourage any policy that would weaken the Allied war effort.
House, Lansing, and Page were so partial to the Allies that
they acted disloyally to the president. Wilson frequently com-
plained about Britain's intolerable course; he sent notes of protest and threatened to do more. He grumbled about Page's
bias for the British and questioned the usefulness of his ambassador in Britain. Yet he did nothing to halt Britain's restrictions on trade with continental Europe, and Page stayed
on in London until the end of the war. Wilson declined to
press the British because he feared that such action would

increase Germany's chances of winning and lead to drastic economic repercussions in the United States. Favoritism for the Allies did not cause the United States to go to war with Germany. It did help create those conditions of 1917 in which war seemed the only choice.

The United States (or much of the population) preferred that Britain and France not collapse, and the nation was equally anxious that Germany not succeed, at least not to the extent of dominating Europe. A prewar suspicion of German militarism and autocratic government, and accounts, during the war, of "uncivilized" German warfare influenced Wilson and a majority of the American people to believe that the United States faced an evil world force, that in going to war with Germany the nation would be striking a blow for liberty and democracy. This general American attitude toward the war of 1914–18 probably influenced Wilson's decision to resist submarine warfare, and thus affected his neutrality policies. More important, it made the decision to intervene seem all the more noble and did much to determine the way the United States, once it became belligerent, prosecuted the war. It was not, however, the major reason for accepting intervention. For all the popular indignation over the invasion of Belgium and other allegedly atrocious German warfare, there still did not develop in the United States a large movement for intervention. Even in 1917 Wilson showed the utmost reluctance to bring the nation into the war. Americans evidently were willing to endure German brutality, although they did not like it, as long as it did not affect their interests; and one must wonder what the American response—and the response of the president—would have been had no Americans been aboard the *Lusitania*. Wilson's vilification on April 2 of the German political system was more a means of sanctifying the cause than a reason for undertaking it. He was a curious crusader. Before April 1917 he would not admit that there was a need for America to take up the sword of righteousness. Against his will he was driven to the barricades, but once he was in the streets he became the most thorough and enthu-siastic of street fighters.

The most important influence on the fate on the United States 1914–17 was the nation's world position. National need and interests were such that it was nearly impossible to avoid the problems which led the nation into war. Even if the ad-ministration had maintained a rigidly neutral position and forced Britain to respect all maritime rights of the United States, it is doubtful that the result would have been different. Grey testified that Britain would have yielded rather than have serious trouble with the United States, which means that, faced with American pressure, Britain would have allowed a larger amount of American trade through to Germany. This was the most the Germans could have expected from the United States, and it would not have affected the contraband trade with the Allies. Germany used submarines not because of the need to obtain American supplies, but from a desire to prevent the Allies from getting them.

The course that would have guaranteed peace for the United States was unacceptable to the American people and the Wilson administration. Only by severing all its European ties could the nation obtain such a guarantee. In 1914 that act would have placed serious strain on an economy that already showed signs of instability; by 1916 it would have been eco-nomically disastrous. At any time it would have been of doubtful political feasibility, even if one were to premise American popular disinterest in who won the war. The British understood this fact and reacted accordingly. If such thoughts suggest that the United States was influenced by the needs of an expanding capitalist economy, so let it be. It is by no means certain that another economic structure would have made much difference.

One might argue that measures short of a total embargo, a different arrangement of neutral practices—for instance, stop-page of the munitions traffic, and/or a ban on American travel on belligerent ships—would have allowed a profitable, humane, yet nonprovocative trade with Europe. Though a reply to that contention can offer no stronger claim to truth than the contention itself, one can offer these points: Wilson argued that yielding one concession on the seas ultimately would lead to pressure to abandon all rights. The pragmatic behavior of belligerents, especially the Germans, makes that assessment seem fair. Lest the German chancellor appear a hero to opponents of American intervention, it is well to remember that Bethmann's views on submarine warfare were not fashioned by love of the United States, or by the agony of knowing his submarines were sending innocent victims to their death. He was guided by simple national interest and the desire to use submarines as fully as circumstances allowed. It also is worth noting that Germany, when it reopened submarine warfare in 1917, was interested not merely in sinking munitions ships, but wanted to prevent all products going to Britain and was especially anxious to halt shipments of food. Had the United States wished to consider Bryan's proposals, keeping people and property out of the danger zone, it would have been easier early in the war, perhaps in February 1915, than after the sinkings began, and above all after the *Lusitania* went down. Yielding in the midst of the *Lusitania* crisis involved nothing short of national humiliation. If Bryan's proposals would have eliminated the sort of incident that provoked intervention, they also would have required a huge sacrifice—too great, as it turned out, for Wilson to accept. The United States would have faced economic loss, loss of national prestige, and probably the eventual prospect of a Europe dominated by Hindenburg, Ludendorff, and Wilhelm II.

No less than the nation as a whole, Wilson found himself accountable for the world standing of the United States. He felt a need and an obligation to promote economic interests abroad. When dealing with Germany he usually spoke in terms of principle; in relations with the Allies he showed awareness of practical considerations. In the hectic days of August 1914, he took steps to get American merchant ships back to sea. In the summer of 1915, advisers alerted him to the financial strain Britain had come to experience, the weakening of the pound sterling and the need to borrow funds in the United States. The secretary of the treasury recommended approval of foreign loans. "To maintain our prosperity we must finance it," he said.[1] Lansing, who believed similarly, wrote the president: "If the European countries cannot find the means to pay for the excess of goods sold them over those purchased from them, they will have to stop buying and our present export trade will shrink proportionately. The result will be restriction of output, industrial depression, idle capital, idle labor, numerous failures, financial demoralization, and general unrest and suffering among the laboring masses." [2] Shortly afterward the administration acquiesced as the House of Morgan floated loans of $500 million for the British and French governments. War traffic with the Allies prompted the German attempt to stop it with submarines. Submarine warfare led to destruction of property and loss of American lives. What had started as efforts to promote prosperity and neutral rights developed into questions of national honor and prestige. Wilson faced not merely the possibility of abandoning economic rights but the humiliating prospect of allowing the Germans to force him to it. The more hazardous it became to exercise American rights, the more difficult it was to yield them.

Wilson's definition of right and honor was itself conditioned by the fact that he was president of the United States and not some less powerful nation. His estimate of what rights belonged to the United States, what was for belligerents fair and humane warfare, rested not simply on a statement of principle, but on the power of the United States to compel observance of these principles. He could not send demands to the German government without some reason for believing the Germans would obey. Interpretation of national honor varies with national economic and military strength. The more powerful the nation, the more the world expects of it and the more the nation expects of itself. Such small seafaring states as

1. Aug. 21, 1915, cited in Link, *The Struggle for Neutrality,* 621.
2. Sept. 6, 1916, *The Lansing Papers,* I, 144–47.

Denmark and the Netherlands suffered extensive losses from submarine warfare, and yet these governments did not feel themselves honor bound to declare war. Wilson credited his right
to act as a mediator to his position as leader of the most
powerful neutral state. Indeed, he sometimes felt obligated to
express moral principle. He could not, and would not, have
acted these ways had he been, let us say, president of the
Dominican Republic. It is thus possible to say that despite
Wilson's commanding personality, his heavy-handedness in
foreign policy and flair for self-righteousness, American
diplomacy in final analysis was less a case of the man guiding
affairs of the nation than the nation, and belligerent nations,
guiding the affairs of the man.

It is tempting to conclude that inasmuch as the United
States was destined to enter the conflict, it might as well have
accepted that fact and reacted accordingly. Presumably this
response would have involved an earlier declaration of war,
certainly a large and rapid rearmament program. In recent
years some "realist" scholars, notably George F. Kennan,
have considered that this course would have been practical.
However wise that policy might have been, it did not fit conditions of the period of neutrality. Wilson opposed entering the
war earlier, and had he thought differently, popular and congressional support were highly questionable. People did not
know in 1914 that commercial relations would lead them into
the World War; most of them believed during the entire period that they could have trade and peace at the same time. The
body of the United States was going one way during the period
of neutrality, its heart and mind another. For a declaration of
war there needed to be a merging of courses.

Then, too, it was not absolutely certain that the United
States had to enter the conflict, for the nation after all did avoid
intervention for over two and one-half years, two-thirds of the
war's fighting time. That same strength which eventually
brought the nation into the war for a while helped it avoid
intervention. From this perspective the campaign for mediation might have represented some of Wilson's soundest think-

ing. German officials never were certain about American strength, and the longer they had to endure a costly, indecisive conflict, the more they were willing to consider the type of gamble taken in 1917. American intervention was all but certain unless the United States made a drastic change in policy —which, as we have seen, it was unwilling to do—or unless someone beforehand brought the war to an end. It incidentally also seems fair to say that an indecisive settlement, a "peace without victory," would have better served the interests of the United States, not to mention the interests of the world, than the vindictive treaty drawn up in 1919. These thoughts, of course, are hindsight, but it is ironic that Wilson made the same observations weeks before the United States entered the war.

Why did the peace effort fail? In some small measure it was due to Wilson's inability to maintain the loyalty of his advisers. House, Page, and Lansing helped convince the Allies that Wilson did not intend to bring to bear on them the tremendous power at his disposal. The movement failed in 1917 largely because American power was not clearly observable to the German government. A better indication of American might, a military force visibly large enough to ensure German defeat, probably would have prevented resumption of submarine warfare and forced the Germans to negotiate. Thus, perhaps the major weakness of Wilson's war policies was an unwillingness to promote a more vigorous preparedness campaign. Even these thoughts are speculative, based on the assumption that Wilson could have done as he wished. Rearmament was no easy burden to impose upon the American people, and even if the United States had possessed a formidable force, there is no way to tell what it would have done with it. Huge armies can be a deterrent to war; they also can hasten its coming.

One of the most provocative features of Wilsonian diplomacy was the president's apparent obsession with moral principle and international law. To critics this tendency suggested blindness to realistic goals, ignorance of the way na-

tions deal with one another, if not a profession of personal
superiority. In some ways the critics were right. Wilson was
dedicated to principle. He thought the old system of interstate
relations was unsatisfactory and looked to a time when nations
would find rules to govern relations among themselves no less
effective than laws within individual states. He wished to have
a large part in making those rules. His propensity to quibble
about shipments of cargo and techniques of approaching ships
at sea seemed a ridiculous and remote abstraction at a time
when the fate of nations hung in balance. It was naïve to expect nations to respect legal principles when they had so much
at stake. If they obeyed Wilson's command, their obedience
was due less to principle than to his nation's ability to retaliate.
At the same time international law was to Wilson more than
an ideal; it was a manifestation of neutral intent and a device
for defining American neutrality. Unless the United States
decided to declare war or to stay out of the mess entirely, it
would have to deal with complicated questions of neutral
rights. International law was not merely convenient, it was the
only device available. There fortunately was no conflict between Wilsonian principle and American rights and needs—
the principle could be used to uphold the need. That the
United States found an attraction for international law is not
surprising: the restraints the law placed on belligerents would
benefit any nation wishing to engage in neutral wartime commerce. International law looked to an orderly international
society, and the United States, a satisfied nation, would profit
from order. The chaos of 1914–17 strengthened feeling in the
United States that American interests coincided with world
interests, or, put another way, that what was good for the
United States was good for the world.

Even so, it is not adequate to say that Wilson was a realist who clothed practical considerations with moral rhetoric.
He was both practical and idealistic, at least during the period
of American neutrality. If he believed that upholding principle would advance American interests, he also hoped that

promoting American interests would serve the cause of international morality. By demonstrating that the United States would not condone brutality, disorder, and lawlessness, he hoped to set a standard for other nations to follow. Wilson wanted to help reform the world, but he would have settled for protecting the interests of the United States and keeping the nation at peace.

Evidence from various quarters supports these final conclusions: there is no indication that Wilson went to war to protect American loans to the Allies and large business interests, although these interests, and economic factors in general, helped bring the United States to a point where war seemed unavoidable.[3] There is no evidence that Wilson asked for war to prevent the defeat of Britain and France. It could well have been, as several scholars have written, that preservation of Britain and France was vital to the interests of the United States. American neutrality, incidentally or by design, functioned to sustain that thesis. Even so, Wilson did not intervene to prevent these nations' collapse; the Allies, while not winning, were not on the verge of losing in the spring of 1917. Nor did Wilson go to war to preserve American security. This is not to say that he was not concerned with security; he simply did not see it in jeopardy. The president did ask his countrymen for war as a means of protecting American honor, rights, and general interest—for both moral and practical reasons. He saw no contradiction between the two. But Wilson's idea of right and interest grew out of what the nation was at the time, and the First World War made clear what had been true for some years: the United States was in all respects a part of the world, destined to profit from its riches and suffer from its woes.

3. This statement and the one which follows takes into account charges later made by revisionists that Wilson's decision for war was influenced by American financiers and businesssmen. These capitalists allegedly feared that unless the United States intervened to save Britain and France, their loans to these nations and the huge market for munitions would be lost.

Appendix

President Wilson's Speech Calling for a Declaration of War Against Germany, April 2, 1917[1]

I have called the Congress into extraordinary session because there are serious, very serious, choices of policy to be made, and made immediately, which it was neither right nor constitutionally permissible that I should assume the responsibility of making.

On the third of February last I officially laid before you the extraordinary announcement of the Imperial German Government that on and after the first day of February it was its purpose to put aside all restraints of law or of humanity and use its submarines to sink every vessel that sought to approach either the ports of Great Britain and Ireland or the western coasts of Europe or any of the ports controlled by the enemies of Germany within the Mediterranean. That had seemed to be the object of the German submarine warfare earlier in the war, but since April of last year the Imperial Government had somewhat restrained the commanders of its undersea craft in conformity with its promise then given to us that passenger boats should not be sunk and that due warning would be given to all other vessels which its submarines might seek to destroy, when no resistance was offered or escape attempted, and care taken that their crews were given at least a fair chance to save their lives in their open boats. The precautions taken were meagre and haphazard enough, as was proved in distressing instance after instance in the progress of the cruel and unmanly business, but a certain degree of restraint was observed. The new policy has swept every restriction aside. Vessels of every

1. Source: *For. Rels., 1917, Supp. I,* 195–203.

kind, whatever their flag, their character, their cargo, their destination, their errand, have been ruthlessly sent to the bottom without warning and without thought of help or mercy for those on board, the vessels of friendly neutrals along with those of belligerents. Even hospital ships and ships carrying relief to the sorely bereaved and stricken people of Belgium, though the latter were provided with safe-conduct through the proscribed areas by the German Government itself and were distinguished by unmistakable marks of identity, have been sunk with the same reckless lack of compassion or of principle.

I was for a little while unable to believe that such things would in fact be done by any government that had hitherto subscribed to the human practices of civilized nations. International law had its origin in the attempt to set up some law which would be respected and observed upon the seas, where no nation had right of dominion and where lay the free highways of the world. By painful stage after stage has that law been built up, with meagre enough results, indeed, after all was accomplished that could be accomplished, but always with a clear view, at least, of what the heart and conscience of mankind demanded. This minimum of right the German Government has swept aside under the plea of retaliation and necessity and because it had no weapons which it could use at sea except these which it is impossible to employ as it is employing them without throwing to the winds all scruples of humanity or of respect for the understandings that were supposed to underlie the intercourse of the world. I am not now thinking of the loss of property involved, immense and serious as that is, but only of the wanton and wholesale destruction of the lives of noncombatants, men, women, and children, engaged in pursuits which have always, even in the darkest periods of modern history, been deemed innocent and legitimate. Property can be paid for; the lives of peaceful and innocent people can not be. The present German submarine warfare against commerce is a warfare against mankind.

It is a war against all nations. American ships have been sunk, American lives taken, in ways which it has stirred us very deeply to learn of, but the ships and people of other neutral and friendly nations have been sunk and overwhelmed in the waters in the same way. There has been no discrimination. The challenge is to all mankind. Each nation must decide for itself how it will meet it.

The choice we make for ourselves must be made with a moderation of counsel and a temperateness of judgment befitting our character and our motives as a nation. We must put excited feeling away. Our motive will not be revenge or the victorious assertion of the physical might of the nation, but only the vindication of right, of human right, of which we are only a single champion.

When I addressed the Congress on the twenty-sixth of February last, I thought that it would suffice to assert our neutral rights with arms, our right to use the seas against unlawful interference, our right to keep our people safe against unlawful violence. But armed neutrality, it now appears, is impracticable. Because submarines are in effect outlaws when used as the German submarines have been used against merchant shipping, it is impossible to defend ships against their attacks as the law of nations has assumed that merchantmen would defend themselves against privateers or cruisers, visible craft giving them chase upon the open sea. It is common prudence in such circumstances, grim necessity indeed, to endeavor to destroy them before they have shown their own intention. They must be dealt with upon sight, if dealt with at all. The German Government denies the right of neutrals to use arms at all within the areas of the sea which it has proscribed, even in the defense of rights which no modern publicist has ever before questioned their right to defend. The intimation is conveyed that the armed guards which we have placed on our merchant ships will be treated as beyond the pale of law and subject to be dealt with as pirates would be. Armed neutrality is ineffectual enough at best; in such circumstances and in the face of such pretensions it is worse than ineffectual; it is likely only to produce what it was meant to prevent; it is practically certain to draw us into the war without either the rights or the effectiveness of belligerents. There is one choice we can not make, we are incapable of making: we will not choose the path of submission and suffer the most sacred rights of our nation and our people to be ignored or violated. The wrongs against which we now array ourselves are no common wrongs; they cut to the very roots of human life.

With a profound sense of the solemn and even tragical character of the step I am taking and of the grave responsibilities which it involves, but in unhesitating obedience to what I deem my constitutional duty, I advise that the Congress declare the recent course of the Imperial German Government to be in fact nothing less than war against the Government and people of the United States; that it formally accept the status of belligerent which has thus been thrust upon it; and that it take immediate steps not only to put the country in a more thorough state of defense but also to exert all its power and employ all its resources to bring the Government of the German Empire to terms and end the war.

What this will involve is clear. It will involve the utmost practicable cooperation in counsel and action with the governments now at war with Germany, and, as incident to that, the extension to those governments of the most liberal financial credits, in order that our resources may so far as possible be added to theirs. It will involve the organization and mobilization of all the material resources of the country to supply the materials of war and serve the incidental needs of the nation in the most abundant and yet the most economical and efficient way possible. It will involve the immediate full equipment of the Navy in all respects but particularly in supplying it with the best means of dealing with the enemy's submarines. It will involve the immediate addition to the armed forces of the United States already provided for by law in case of war at least 500,000 men who should, in my opinion, be chosen upon the principle of universal liability to service, and also the authorization of subsequent additional increments of equal force so soon as they may be needed and can be handled in training. It will involve also, of course, the granting of adequate credits to the Government, sustained, I hope, so far as they can equitably be sustained by the present generation, by well conceived taxation.

I say sustained so far as may be equitable by taxation because it seems to me that it would be most unwise to base the credits which will now be necessary entirely on money borrowed. It is our duty, I most respectfully urge, to protect our people so far as we may against the very serious hardships and evils which would be likely to arise out of the inflation which would be produced by vast loans.

In carrying out the measures by which these things are to be accomplished we should keep constantly in mind the wisdom of interfering as little as possible in our own preparation and in the equipment of our own military forces with the duty—for it will be a very practical duty—of supplying the nations already at war with Germany with the materials which they can obtain only from us or by our assistance. They are in the field and we should help them in every way to be effective there.

I shall take the liberty of suggesting, through the several executive departments of the Government, for the consideration of your committees, measures for the accomplishment of the several objects I have mentioned. I hope that it will be your pleasure to deal with them as having been framed after very careful thought by the branch of the Government upon which the responsibility of conducting the war and safeguarding the nation will most directly fall.

While we do these things, these deeply momentous things, let us be very clear, and make very clear to all the world what our motives and our objects are. My own thought has not been driven from its habitual and normal course by the unhappy events of the last two months, and I do not believe that the thought of the nation has been altered or clouded by them. I have exactly the same things in mind now that I had in mind when I addressed the Senate on the twenty-second of January last, the same that I had in mind when I addressed the Congress on the third of February and on the twenty-sixth of February. Our object now, as then, is to vindicate the principles of peace and justice in the life of the world as against selfish and autocratic power and to set up amongst the really free and self-governed peoples of the world such a concert of purpose and of action as will henceforth ensure the observance of those principles. Neutrality is no longer feasible or desirable where the peace of the world is involved and the freedom of its peoples, and the menace to that peace and freedom lies in the existence of autocratic governments backed by organized force which is controlled wholly by their will, not by the will of their people. We have seen the last of neutrality in such circumstances. We are at the beginning of an age in which it will be insisted that the same standards of conduct and of responsibility for wrong done shall be observed among nations and their governments that are observed among the individual citizens of civilized states.

We have no quarrel with the German people. We have no feeling towards them but one of sympathy and friendship. It was not upon their impulse that their Government acted in entering this war. It was not with their previous knowledge or approval. It was a war determined upon as wars used to be determined upon in the old, unhappy days when peoples were nowhere consulted by their rulers and wars were provoked and waged in the interest of dynasties or of little groups of ambitious men who were accustomed to use their fellow men as pawns and tools. Self-governed nations do not fill their neighbour states with spies or set the course of intrigue to bring about some critical posture of affairs which will give them an opportunity to strike and make conquest. Such designs can be successfully worked out only under cover and where no one has the right to ask questions. Cunningly contrived plans of deception or aggression, carried, it may be, from generation to generation, can be worked out and kept from the light only within the privacy of courts or behind the carefully guarded confidences of a narrow and privileged class. They are happily impossible where public opinion commands and insists upon full information concerning all the nation's affairs.

A steadfast concert for peace can never be maintained except by a partnership of democratic nations. No autocratic government could be trusted to keep faith within it or observe its covenants. It must be a league of honour, a partnership of opinion. Intrigue would eat its vitals away; the plottings of inner circles who could plan what they would and render account to no one would be a corruption seated at its very heart. Only free peoples can hold their purpose and their honour steady to a common end and prefer the interests of mankind to any narrow interest of their own.

Does not every American feel that assurance has been added to our hope for the future peace of the world by the wonderful and heartening things that have been happening within the last few weeks in Russia? Russia was known by those who knew it best to have been always in fact democratic at heart, in all the vital habits of her thought, in all the intimate relationships of her people that spoke their natural instinct, their habitual attitude towards life. The autocracy that crowned the summit of her political structure, long as it had stood and terrible as was the reality of its power, was not in fact Russian in origin, character, or purpose; and now it has been shaken off and the great, generous Russian people have been added in all their naive majesty and might to the forces that are fighting for freedom in the world, for justice, and for peace. Here is a fit partner for a league of honour.

One of the things that has served to convince us that the Prussian autocracy was not and could never be our friend is that from the very outset of the present war it has filled our unsuspecting communities and even our offices of government with spies and set criminal intrigues everywhere afoot against our national unity of counsel, our peace within and without, our industries and our commerce. Indeed it is now evident that its spies were here even before the war began; and it is unhappily not a matter of conjecture but a fact proved in our courts of justice that the intrigues which have more than once come perilously near to disturbing the peace and dislocating the industries of the country have been carried on at the instigation, with the support, and even under the personal direction of official agents of the Imperial Government accredited to the Government of the United States. Even in checking these things and trying to extirpate them we have sought to put the most generous interpretation possible upon them because we knew that their source lay, not in any hostile feeling or purpose of the German people towards us (who were, do doubt, as ignorant of them as we ourselves were), but only in the selfish designs of a Government that did what it pleased and told its people nothing. But they have played their part in serving to convince us at last that that Government entertains no real friendship for us and means to act against our peace and security at its convenience. That it means to stir up enemies against us at our very doors the intercepted note to the German Minister at Mexico City is eloquent evidence.

We are accepting this challenge of hostile purpose because we know that in such a government, following such methods, we can never have a friend; and that in the presence of its organized power, always lying in wait to accomplish we know not what purpose, there can be no assured security for the democratic governments of the world. We are now about to accept gage of battle with this natural foe to liberty and shall, if necessary, spend the whole force of the nation to check and nullify its pretensions and its power. We are glad, now that we see the facts with no veil of false pretense about them, to fight thus for the ultimate peace of the world and for the liberation of its peoples, the German peoples included: the the rights of nations great and small and the privilege of men everywhere to choose their way of life and of obedience. The world must be made safe for democracy. Its peace must be planted upon the tested foundations of political liberty. We have no selfish ends to serve. We desire no conquest, no domination for the sacrifices we shall freely make. We are but one of the champions of the rights of mankind. We shall be satisfied when those rights have been made as secure as the faith and the freedom of nations can make them.

Just because we fight without rancour and without selfish object, seeking nothing for ourselves but what we shall wish to share with all free peoples, we shall, I feel confident, conduct our operations as belligerents without passion and ourselves observe with proud punctilio the principles of right and of fair play we profess to be fighting for.

I have said nothing of the governments allied with the Imperial Government of Germany because they have not made war upon us or challenged us to defend our right and our honour. The Austro-Hungarian Government has, indeed, avowed its unqualified endorsement and acceptance of the reckless and lawless submarine warfare adopted now without disguise by the Imperial German Government, and it has therefore not been possible for this Government to receive Count Tarnowski, the Ambassador recently accredited to this Government by the Imperial and Royal Government of Austria-Hungary; but that Government has not actually engaged in warfare against citizens of the United States on the seas, and I take the liberty, for the present at least, of postponing a discussion of our relations with the authorities at Vienna. We enter this war only where we are clearly forced into it because there are no other means of defending our rights.

It will be all the easier for us to conduct ourselves as belligerents in a high spirit of right and fairness because we act without animus, not in enmity towards a people or with the desire to bring any injury or disadvantage upon them, but only in armed opposition to an irresponsible government which has thrown aside all considerations of humanity and of right and is running amuck. We are, let me say again, the sincere friends of the German people, and shall desire nothing so much as the early reestablishment of intimate relations of mutual advantage between us—however hard it may be for them, for the time being, to believe that this is spoken from our hearts. We have borne with their present government through all these bitter months because of that friendship—exercising a patience and forbearance which would otherwise have been impossible. We shall, happily, still have an opportunity to prove that friendship in our daily attitude and actions towards the millions of men and women of German birth and native sympathy who live amongst us and share our life, and we shall be proud to prove it towards all who are in fact loyal to their neighbours and to the Government in the hour of test. They are, most of them, as true and loyal Americans as if they had never known any other fealty or allegiance. They will be prompt to stand with us in rebuking and restraining the few who may be of a different mind and purpose. If there should be disloyalty, it will be dealt with with a firm hand of stern repression; but if it lifts its head at all, it will lift it only here and there and without countenance except from a lawless and malignant few.

It is a distressing and oppressive duty, gentlemen of the Congress, which I have performed in thus addressing you. There are, it may be, many months of fiery trial and sacrifice ahead of us. It is a fearful thing to lead this great peaceful people into war, into the most terrible and disastrous of all wars, civilization itself seeming to be in the balance. But the right is more precious than peace, and we shall fight for the things which we have always carried nearest our hearts—for democracy, for the right of those who submit to authority to have a voice in their own governments, for the rights and liberties of small nations, for a universal dominion of right by such a concert of free peoples as shall bring peace and safety to all nations and make the world itself at last free. To such a task we can dedicate our lives and our fortunes, everything that we are and everything that we have, with the pride of those who know that the day has come when America is privileged to spend her blood and her might for the principles that gave her birth and happiness and the peace which she has treasured. God helping her, she can do no other.

Bibliographic Essay

THIS ESSAY has a twofold purpose: to give credit to the sources —not always cited in the footnotes—helpful in the preparation of this volume; to provide, for the reader's reference, a survey of published works dealing with aspects of the background to American intervention in the First World War. The essay does not offer a complete list of publications but includes only those works found to be most helpful, up to date, or representative of a point of view.

Private Papers and Government Collections

While virtually all the government records and private manuscript collections bearing on this period are open to public scrutiny, a few are of special merit. These collections include the private papers of House and Frank L. Polk at the Yale Library, the papers of Page at Harvard, the papers of Wilson and Lansing in the Library of Congress, the mammoth collection of State Department papers in the National Archives in Washington, the records of the British Foreign Office and personal papers of Edward Grey, Arthur Balfour, Lord Robert Cecil and Sir Cecil Spring-Rice in the Public Record Office in London.

One also should make special mention of two published primary materials easily available to students who wish to research the First World War: the excellent documentary collection published by the State Department, *Foreign Relations of the United States, Supplements, 1914–1920,* and the *New York Times* for the period 1914–17, which gave remarkably thorough coverage of national and world events.

Biographies and Diplomatic Biographies

For all the interest in Woodrow Wilson, no one yet has written an up-to-date single-volume biography short enough to be manageable—three hundred or so pages—and long enough to give decent coverage to the man and his presidency. There are, however, several good works of various length. Short studies include a volume by *John A. Garraty, *Woodrow Wilson* (New York, 1956), and by *John M. Blum, *Woodrow Wilson and the Politics of Morality* (Boston, 1956). Wilsonian historiography received a sharp new twist in 1967 with publication of *Thomas Woodrow Wilson: A Psychological Study* (Boston, 1967) by Sigmund Freud and William C. Bullitt. The authors, a retired American diplomat and the famous Viennese psychiatrist, did not give Wilson a very friendly treatment. What Freud and Bullitt did was to take striking Wilsonian characteristics and carry them to the most distasteful extreme, and to find other personality traits which most scholars deny existed. The authors found Wilson neurotic, effeminate, oblivious to any opinion but his own. Students of Wilson have found the book of remarkable interest and highly questionable validity. Some of the sharpest criticism by Freud and Bullitt has been challenged by two recent scholarly books on aspects of Wilson's life: George C. Osborn, *Woodrow Wilson: The Early Years* (Baton Rouge, La., 1968), and Henry W. Bragdon, *Woodrow Wilson: The Academic Years* (Cambridge, Mass., 1967). Longer studies of Wilson include the old authorized biography by Ray Stannard Baker, *Woodrow Wilson: Life and Letters* (8 vols., Garden City, N.Y., 1927–39), the volumes of which vary in quality; and *Arthur Walworth, *Woodrow Wilson* (2 vols., Boston, 1958). Walworth's books are highly readable and highly favorable to Wilson. Volume One has as its subtitle *American Prophet,* and Volume Two *World Prophet.* The present in-depth biographer of Wilson is Arthur S. Link, whose massive, exhaustively researched study now has reached five volumes and the time of American intervention into the World War. The first two volumes, **The Road to the White House* (Princeton, N.J., 1947) and **The New Freedom* (Princeton, N.J., 1956) cover Wilson's early life and establishment of his presidential administration. The last three, *The Struggle for Neutrality, 1914–1915* (Princeton, N.J., 1960); *Confusions and Crises, 1915–1916* (Princeton, N.J., 1964); and *Campaigns for Progressivism and Peace, 1916–1917* (Princeton, N.J., 1965) focus on the background to intervention. In some ways these books constitute much more than a

* Available in paperback.

biography; in some ways they are less. They give remarkably detailed coverage of decisions in the American government and—perhaps more striking—in belligerent governments. On the other hand, they offer little about Wilson's personal life, and are less a biography of Wilson than a study of his times. Two other books, not exactly biographies but appropriate to this study are Link's *Wilson the Diplomatist: A Look at His Major Foreign Policies* (Baltimore, 1957), and the older but still highly regarded *Origins of the Foreign Policy of Woodrow Wilson* (Baltimore, 1937), by Harley Notter.

Oddly enough, there is no decent biography of Colonel House. One reason is that most studies of Wilson indirectly have been studies of House, and a book about the Colonel would have to repeat much of what is already said in books about Wilson. Another reason is the multivolume work edited by Charles Seymour, *The Intimate Papers of Colonel House* (4 vols., Boston, 1926–28). A highly successful and important publication, these volumes combined biographical narrative with excerpts from House's diaries and letters. Seymour treated his subject in a very favorable, almost flawless tone, and the volumes will not stand as objective biography. There is also *Alexander L. and Juliette George, *Woodrow Wilson and Colonel House: A Personality Study* (New York, 1956), a sort of predecessor to the Freud book (though not nearly as unflattering), which treats the relations between these two men in an interesting way.

The older studies of Bryan have been superseded by Lawrence W. Levine's *Defender of the Faith: William Jennings Bryan, the Last Decade, 1915–1925* (New York, 1965), and Paolo Coletta's *William Jennings Bryan* (3 vols., Lincoln, Neb., 1965–69). Coletta's last two volumes, *Progressive Politician and Moral Statesman, 1909–1915* and *Political Puritan, 1915–1925,* both published in 1969, treat Bryan and the World War. The author was much impressed with Bryan's contribution to foreign policy and the soundness of his ideas on neutrality.

The contemporary scholar of Robert Lansing is Daniel M. Smith, author of *Robert Lansing and American Neutrality 1914–1917* (Berkeley, Calif., 1958) and "Robert Lansing and the Formation of American Neutrality Policies, 1914–1915," *Mississippi Valley Historical Review,* XLIII (June 1956), 59–81. Smith finds

Lansing to be a diplomatic realist and an important man in foreign policy, much responsible for neutrality policies in 1914–15. Coletta makes some of the same claims for Bryan. Lansing's volume, *War Memoirs of Robert Lansing* (Indianapolis, 1935) is of use, for it points out objectives of the secretary's diplomacy (to help the Allies win the war) and includes important memoranda written during the war.

Works on other individuals include Burton J. Hendrick, *The Life and Letters of Walter Hines Page* (3 vols., Garden City, N.Y., 1924–26). These volumes contain many of Page's letters from London, surely some of the most exciting written during the war. Page's letters advance the most pronounced pro-Ally bias of any American, a view fully endorsed by author Hendrick. A considerably revised assessment of Page comes in a recent study by Ross Gregory, *Walter Hines Page: Ambassador to the Court of St. James's* (Lexington, Ky., 1970). For coverage of militant criticism of Wilson's policy see John A. Garraty, *Henry Cabot Lodge* (New York, 1953), and two books on Roosevelt: **Theodore Roosevelt* (New York, 1931) by Henry Pringle, a fascinating, sharply critical, Pulitzer Prize winner, and the newer, balanced account by *William Henry Harbaugh, Power and Responsibility: The Life and Times of Theodore Roosevelt* (New York, 1961). Pacifist objection to American policy comes out in the volumes of Levine and Coletta on Bryan, and in Belle Case and Fola La Follette, *Robert M. LaFollette, June 14, 1885–June 18, 1925* (2 vols., New York, 1953).

Studies of officials in belligerent governments have not been as numerous as books on Americans. In fact the best coverage of events in Berlin, Paris, and London appears in works on American diplomacy. There are, however, a few studies of value. The most important is Viscount Grey of Fallodon (Sir Edward Grey), *Twenty-five Years, 1892–1916* (2 vols., New York, 1925), by the British foreign secretary, which usually (but not always) gives a candid view of Britain's policy toward the United States. Another useful study is George M. Trevelyan, *Grey of Fallodon* (Boston, 1937), which benefited from early access to some of the files of the Foreign Office. Both studies reaffirm Grey's intent to maintain friendly relations with the United States while keeping American trade from Germany. See also Stephen Gwynn, ed., *The Letters and Friendships of Sir Cecil Spring-Rice* (2 vols., London, 1929), and

Johann H. von Bernstorff, *My Three Years in America* (New York, 1920)—both accounts by or concerning ambassadors in the United States. Together with the works on Page, these volumes suggest how much foreign diplomats come under the influence of opinion in the country of their residence. Finally there is the work edited by Walter Goerlitz, *The Kaiser and His Court: The Diaries, Note Books and Letters of Admiral Georg Alexander von Müller, Chief of the Naval Cabinet, 1914–1918* (London, 1961), one of the few original accounts of events within the German government and the emperor's court.

Studies on the Background to Intervention

The starting place for reading about this subject and about the war in general would be the small volume by *Arthur S. Link and William M. Leary, Jr., eds., *The Progressive Era and the Great War 1896–1920* (New York, 1969) an up-to-date bibliography of major books and articles.

The historiography of American intervention has taken many turns, a fact which suggests that there is close relationship between historical interpretation and world and national conditions at the time the books were written. The books most commonly read in the 1920s were Hendrick's volumes on Page and Seymour's on House. Both studies viewed intervention as a wise and necessary act; both suggested that the United States probably should have entered the war earlier. A reconsideration of these assumptions began in the late 1920s, both in public opinion and in books published about the World War. By that time the United States had undergone a great deal of irksome quibbling with its wartime allies, particularly over their unwillingness to pay war debts owed the United States. Moreover, it was obvious that the nation had not accomplished the grand objects for which Wilson had urged intervention. This atmosphere helped give rise to a group of writers who revised or refuted earlier-accepted reasons for intervention. The first "revisionist" book was by C. Hartley Grattan, *Why We Fought* (New York, 1929), which argued that intervention had come as a result of unneutral policies, and was unwise, unnecessary, of no benefit to the United States. The peak of revisionism came in the 1930s, for at that time critics could add new information about war-profiteering to earlier doubts about American policy in 1914–17.

Many people came to accept the thesis that a small group of industrialists and financiers had. maneuvered the United States into war in 1917 to protect the munitions traffic and loans extended the Allies—unworthy reasons indeed. It was, besides, a time of new international tension, when Americans began to fear that the United States might face pressure to enter a second world war, with results no more pleasant than what had come out of the first one. There followed in public policy a series of neutrality acts designed to prevent such a catastrophe. There also followed a large number of revisionist books which varied in length, emphasis, and manner of presentation, but all pointing toward the theme that the United States had made many mistakes in 1914–17, and that if the Wilson administration had avoided these mistakes the nation could, and should, have avoided war. These writings also carried an implicit warning that the nation should do everything possible to prevent a second foolish venture. Walter Millis's *Road to War: America 1914–1917* (Boston, 1935) was a witty, lively volume by a journalist, which stressed British propaganda and other unworthy influences on the United States. So did the scholarly accounts by Edwin M. Borchard and William P. Lage, *Neutrality for the United States* (New Haven, 1937), and H. C. Peterson, *Propaganda for War: The Campaign Against American Neutrality, 1914–1917* (Norman, Oklahoma, 1939). Perhaps the most impressive revisionist study was Charles C. Tansill, *America Goes to War* (Boston, 1938), a massive, sharply critical account that placed emphasis on economic factors and the strong unneutral feelings of Wilson and his advisers. Alice M. Morrissey's *The American Defense of Neutral Rights 1914–1917* (Cambridge, Mass., 1939) was not as personal or opinionated as Tansill's book, but it did argue that Wilson was timid in upholding neutral rights with respect to British policy. Even Ray Stannard Baker, long an admirer of Wilson, offered some doubts about American policy as he published, in the 1930s, the last volumes of his large biography.

In the 1940s and 1950s the issue of intervention was fought out largely as a part of the controversy between "moralist" and "realist" diplomacy. Having experienced a second world conflict, and willing to admit the inevitability of American involvement in world affairs, most writers in this period questioned not the wis-

dom of intervention in 1917, but the reasons for entering and fighting the war. Walter Lippman, the respected journalist and political
commentator, anticipated the new dispute during the war when he
published *United States Foreign Policy: Shield of the Republic*
(Boston, 1943). Lippman argued that for all Wilson's moral
rhetoric the United States had gone to war in 1917 for practical
reasons, to uphold national security. He wrote that the nation in
1917 as in 1941 could not tolerate German control of continental
Europe and the Atlantic Ocean. Lippman then was challenged
(directly or indirectly) by several students of American foreign
policy, notably *George F. Kennan, *American Diplomacy 1900–
1950* (Chicago, 1950); Hans Morgenthau, *In Defense of the National Interest* (New York, 1951); and Robert E. Osgood, *Ideals
and Self-Interest in American Foreign Relations* (Chicago, 1953).
These "realists" argued that while it probably was necessary to
enter the war for purposes of national interest, Wilson had intervened on grounds of abstract moral principles and in defense of
an equally abstract code of international law. The United States
as a result had no concrete objectives for fighting, no foundation
for peace; and Wilsonian diplomacy had set highly undesirable
tones for future American policy. Finally, Edward Buehrig turned
somewhat the other way when he published *Woodrow Wilson and
the Balance of Power* (Bloomington, Ind., 1955). As the title suggests, Buehrig saw Wilson as being much influenced by the realistic
need to maintain the European balance of power. All these writers
fancied themselves advocates of practical, unemotional diplomacy;
they differed in assessing the practicality of Wilson's foreign policy.

The most recent studies of American intervention have sought
to balance the contentions. Such writers as *Ernest R. May, *The
World War and American Isolation: 1914–1917* (Cambridge, Mass.,
1959); and *Arthur S. Link, *Woodrow Wilson and the Progressive
Era: 1910–1917* (New York, 1954), and his recent volumes on
Wilson have found the United States and its president influenced
by many factors, some moral, some practical. Both authors spend
considerable time describing events in belligerent nations and their
impact on the United States. While Link and May express an intent to avoid moral judgment, their writings reflect the authors'
feeling that Wilson's policy was much more correct than incorrect.

For brief coverage of American intervention, one might see

the account in *Daniel M. Smith, *The Great Departure: The United States and World War I, 1914–1920* (New York, 1965), and the same author's interpretive essay, "National Interest and American Intervention, 1917: An Historical Reappraisal," *Journal of American History* LII (June 1965), 5–24. An analysis of revisionist writings appears in Warren I. Cohen, *The American Revisionists: The Lessons of Intervention in World War I* (Chicago, 1967). One can sample the major schools of thought in the booklet *America's Entry into World War I* (New York, 1967), edited by Herbert J. Bass.

Specialized Studies

Students interested in aspects of American policy might wish to consult some of the many studies that concentrate on smaller parts of the problem of intervention. Link's works on Wilson are large and broad enough so that they can give coverage to several issues peripheral to the large theme. On American public opinion there are the well-received books: Cedric Cummins, *Indiana Public Opinion and the World War, 1914–1917* (Indianapolis, 1945); J. C. Crighton, *Missouri and the World War, 1914–1917* (Columbia, Mo., 1947); and Edwin Costrell, *How Maine Viewed the War, 1914–1917* (Orono, Me., 1940). Mark Sullivan describes aspects of the American reaction to neutrality policies and the war in Volume V of his colorful, popularized history, *Our Times: The United States, 1900–1925* (6 vols., New York, 1926–35). The attitude of some congressmen appears in Alex M. Arnett, *Claude Kitchin and the Wilson War Policies* (Boston, 1937). For an important segment of British opinion see Armin Rappaport, *The British Press and Wilsonian Neutrality* (Stanford, Calif., 1951). For critical decisions in Germany see the book by K. E. Birnbaum, *Peace Moves and U Boat Warfare: A Study of Germany's Policy Towards the United States, April 18, 1916–January 9, 1917* (Stockholm, 1958). There is a lively account of the sinking of the *Lusitania* in *A. A. and Mary Hoehling, *The Last Voyage of the Lusitania* (New York, 1956). Technical aspects are covered in Thomas A. Bailey, "The Sinking of the *Lusitania*," *American Historical Review* XLI (Oct., 1935), 54–73. Barbara Tuchman's*The Zimmermann Telegram* (New York, 1958) is skillfully written, but it probably overemphasizes the importance of the telegram.

Other articles of interest include Ross Gregory, "A New Look at the Case of the *Dacia*," *Journal of American History* LX (September 1968), 292–96; Richard W. Van Alstyne, "The Policy of the United States regarding the Declaration of London at the outbreak of the Great War," *Journal of Modern History* VII (December 1933), which one might call a revisionist article; and Jerold S. Auerbach, "Woodrow Wilson's 'Prediction' to Frank Cobb: Words Historians Should Doubt Ever Got Spoken," *Journal of American History* LIV (December 1967), 608–17.

Despite the mountain of literature about this period—and this essay contains only a small portion of it—the subject is not closed. One must suppose that students will continue in the future, as they have in the past, to interpret the Great War in the light of the world around them.

Index